Bus Your Own Table

My Journey to Being the Most Educated Woman in Fast Food

Janetha Luke

PublishAmerica
Baltimore

Hardcover 978-1-4560-0746-1
Softcover 978-1-4560-0747-8
PUBLISHED BY PUBLISHAMERICA, LLLP
www.publishamerica.com
Baltimore

Printed in the United States of America

DEDICATION:

Fellow author, Kim Acrylic, the founder of the feast.
Rosa, Tiff/ Christie for their encouragement.
Renee and Kitty, the last of my spirit daughters.
The AFI fans, even the ones who broke my heart.
Toni, Tori & Steph: mi familia.
My straightedge brothers and sisters here and in the UK.
Kerra, Becky and Joseph, my family in Oklahoma.
~~My best and oldest friend Peej,~~
and my hubby Axl Rosebush,
Toni, Axl Rosebush (my hubby, not his real name) and PJ, you are the only ones who have stood by me all these years. I can never say I love you enough,

Years come and go, but my feelings for you are foREVer.

Sophie!
So happy to have
met you. Thanks for
being my unofficial little
sister.
"Keep the faith
Stay gold
stay true to yourself
x your friends
x never let go!"
Joey JabooK
Samantha
Luke
xxx

ACKNOWLEDGEMENTS:

Kim Acrylic
Donald Brown, who helped me in editing this.

Many names have been changed.

PREFACE

Straight Edge refers to a lifestyle that started in the punk subculture whose adherents make a lifetime commitment to abstain from using alcohol, tobacco, and recreational drugs. The term was coined by Minor Threat in the song "Straight Edge". Straightedge is often symbolized by three Xs, representing the three things abstained from: drugs, alcohol, tobacco and the abbreviation sXe.

"Is your name really Joey?"
"Yes."
"It's not short for anything?"
"No. I was named after my dad."

Carrie Fisher once said that her mother raised her to be a virgin as if it were a high paying profession. My father was Arab so my staying a virgin til my death was pretty much already assumed. I think if there was one thing I learned from my father it was his work ethic. It was nothing he told me or lectured me about the way he lectured me not to do drugs (never have) and stay away from heavy metal music(well, I've never done drugs), it was simply the way he lived. He never rested, he never took a vacation, he never took time off, he barely took the time to eat and that is what probably killed him in the end. He did not work so that we could have a big house, he never drove a new vehicle ever in his life, for him work was its own reward.

My father was a cowboy who adored Ronald Reagan and he would have a meltdown if he could hear me say this but I truly believe my father is the reason I am a Socialist today. He is also the reason I have put myself through sixty hour weeks, filthy conditions, incompetent coworkers and jobs I hated just to have employment.

There were things I did after my dad's death with the sole intention of pissing him off posthumously. One was getting tattooed from head to toe, one was campaigning for and electing our first black President, the third was becoming educated. My father sought no more education than would allow him to run his western wear store and he expected me to have no other aspirations of my own. However I looked around me and because education was the one thing no one in my family gave a damn about, it became my one goal in life. I was convinced (though by what or whom I am not sure) that the key to life was education. I somehow had it in my head that those who were educated were rewarded with good jobs, houses, stability, status in communities. Nothing could be further from the truth. I wasted the first part of my life on education to end up working fast food.

This is how I got there, illustrated through remembrances, narratives, anecdotes, journal entries, poems, and essays of the last twenty five years of my life

CHAPTER 1

I started working for my dad when I was thirteen. I didn't have a choice in the matter, he was not leaving me at home with my abusive step mom who was borderline schizophrenic and completely unhinged. Looking back I'm glad he did because had he not, I would have never gotten to see him at all. I didn't tally how many hours my father worked so I can't tell you if it was sixty hours a week or more or less. It felt like it was. He never took a break, he never took a vacation, he never took a day off, he didn't take lunch breaks. He ate one meal a day, usually late at night, sometime after midnight when he got home. That only happened if my step mother cooked, if there were left overs, and if she wasn't throwing said left overs at him the moment he walked in the door. He usually snuck in a few bites at work but it never constituted an actual meal.

My father ran a small clothing store on a highway. He sold work clothes, coveralls, work boots, jeans, and everything from wedding gowns to christening outfits to housewares. My grandfather never believed in putting anything on sale so walking into the store was like walking into a museum. There were still wedding and prom dresses left over from when it was a department store, back when my grandfather, who built the business was alive. These were right next to authentic sixties bell bottoms and seventies embroidered cowboy shirts and giant western hats with gaudy feathers or concho bands.

Our store was on "The North Side", supposedly the bad part of town, the slum. I never thought much about it growing up because the whole town seemed pretty trashy. But after a while I realized the popular kids lived up on the hill. It was like that cartoon, The Oblongs, where the rich people lived on the hill and breathed the good air, the poor people lived in the valley and breathed the polluted air and were born deformed, missing arms and legs or with two heads. It took me years to realize I was a valley dweller, before I started school I truly believed I was one of the blessed.

CHAPTER 2

Our town was thriving once, there was an Air Force base until the mid-seventies and after that the business of the oil field exploded and brought everyone prosperity. This lasted until sometime in the nineteen eighties. Being a teenager I was too self-absorbed at the time to tell you exactly when it wall went South, but eventually it did and I got a ring side seat to the demise of my father's health and our family business.

Growing up I really believed we were dirt poor. Anything I asked for growing up, a stereo, name brand clothes, a car or whatever, I was told "No, we can't afford that." While all the cool kids wore Esprit and Gloria Vanderbilt and Nike and Guess, I wore the clothing my dad sold: Levi's (long before they were expensive and the "in" thing to wear), Wranglers, cowboy boots. I never realized I was actually raised to be middle class until I took a course on understanding how poverty affects students. I was taught to save, not spend, and to never talk about what you had or didn't have. Though I only saw money twice growing up (and I'll get to that in a bit), what I had no idea we possessed so much of was property. My father made it sound like we were always on the brink of being on the street. Each time I took off my shoes, even indoors, I got yelled at because my father was so sure I was going to get sick and he'd always tell me how he could never afford to take me to a doctor if that happened. When I needed dental work he sent me to the cheapest dentist in town, who was also a quack. In trying to remove a tooth he bruised my mouth and jaw so much that when I returned to school everyone thought my dad had beaten me up.

After my dad died rumors flew about that he had hoarded money and stashed it all over the place: our house, my grandparent's house, the clothing store. This was actually honestly true, however that money went to serve a purpose. My sisters on my mom's side were convinced I was keeping this loot to myself and not sharing with them. One went so far as to call the others, lie and say she had seen me removing a large chest (what a cliché) from one of our liquidation sales and that it had been full of money. She then called me, demanding her share. What money there had been was gone, because my father was a good man.

One time, when I was very, very young, probably six years old, I was over at my Grandma Jabor's house. This was back when both grandparents were still alive. My grandparents on my father's side spoke only Spanish and Arabic. Being a child and having no idea what they were saying and not being able to communicate with them scared me to death so I stayed away from that place when at all possible. Still, that day some of our relatives were down from El Paso and I was there with my father. As I went through the house I spied one of my much, much older cousins. He was sitting at a table piled with money. The only way I can describe it is like seeing Scrooge McDuck in the old Disney cartoons. There were stacks of coins and stacks of bills and he was busy counting them and didn't even look up. Within moments it was clear I was not supposed to have seen that as dad steered me into the other room quite fast, but it was too late. I'm sure the look on my face said everything.

My dad took me aside and said in a conspiratorial tone: "You cannot tell anyone ever about seeing that money. I'm going to tell you a secret. Your cousin Miled has a gambling problem. All that money is owed to someone very dangerous. Your cousin is counting it before he gives it back. Your Mama and Papa don't know about it. If they knew it would break their hearts. If anyone else ever found out about it your cousin could be killed. You can never ever tell anyone else you saw this."

I'm sure my eyes were as big as saucers as I swallowed it hook, line and sinker and promised my dad I would never open my mouth and actually promptly forgot it all until I was in my thirties!

In the back of my dad's store there was a stock room CRAMMED full from floor to rafters with junk: boots, winter clothes, prom dresses from the fifties, wedding gowns from the seventies, hats, hangers, and god knows what else. The first thing you would see upon going back there was a large wooden table meant for packing, wrapping and mailing. When my sister Toni and I were in school and our friends would come to visit, we would give them a black magic marker and have them sign the table top. The back of the table held a role of butcher's paper or brown wrap or Christmas wrap, depending on the occasion.

One day I came home from college, in what we would not know then was the late stages of my dad's illness, to find the entire table covered in stacks of paper money. I do not recall any specific denomination, but I do know the stacks were more than two or three inches high, there were multiple stacks and so many of them all over the table that you could not see any part of the wooden table or black scribbles. Many things did not occur to me in those days because I was in the grips of literally watching my father waste away and die right in front of me. It didn't occur to me to go poking around in it and for once Dad, for whom almost everything was "hands off!" didn't tell me to stay the hell away from it. If I looked at it closely or tried to estimate it's value I have long since forgotten, the sight of my father, a living skeleton on his death bed having wipe away almost all other memories of the time. It turned out that he had taken out tens of thousands of dollars in loans to keep the clothing store going. The money on the table went to pay it all back. He knew he was dying, he knew he was going to leave my sister and I with nearly eighty thousand dollars of hospital bills and he'd be damned if he was going to saddle us with the debt from the store too.

So yes, the rumors were true, it turned out we were rich, but the money actually went for debts which is more than I can say for the people who borrowed from him. I was attending a Pentecostal church when he died and had been since I was fourteen. Several prominent members of this church came to my father's store, bought work clothes for themselves and their employees on credit and never paid it back. When he died I wrote to one of their wives and asked her to find charity in her heart to do her Christian duty and ask her husband to make good on the debt to help pay for my father's funeral. I will call her Sister Grimm. If I printed her name here, being the paragon of Christian virtue that she was, I know she would sue me. Sister Grimm's husband had a funny nickname...fatty or pokey or something like that. He was successful in the oil field and sent his employees to buy work clothes and work boots on credit, never paying him back. What would a good Christian woman do? Come to our store and send her deepest sympathies on my loss? Ask her husband to take up a collection for my Dad's funeral? Send flowers? Yes, a good Christian woman would do all these things. What did Sister Grimm do? She came to our store, threw the note in my face and cussed me out. No one ever paid my dad back, not one dime. My sister and I paid for the funeral ourselves.

On a side note, twenty years later I found Sister Grimm's son on facebook. Since we had gone to Bible school together I sent him a friends request. He accepted it and promptly spammed my walls with anti-Middle Eastern racial slurs and called me a terrorist. The apple didn't fall far from the tree. It never does.

My dad was one of a kind. I know I got my mom's intelligence and passive aggressiveness and my dad's twisted sense of humor. Dad referred to gays as "them funny boys". We never once had a conversation about love, sex or dating, the mysteries of growing into a woman I was left to discover from books, magazines and television. Everything I needed to know I learned from Judith Krantz! My dad was obviously raised to have such a mental block as sex being something you did not discuss—at least with your teenage daughter. The one and only time he was forced to confront it was a memory I'll never forget.

We had an old fat television in the store where I and the only other person Dad trusted enough to work with him, Angelina Hernandez would watch soap operas during the day. It only got in one channel, we were stuck with NBC. Dad never watched except to pause a brief moment if pro wrestling was on ("What are them clowns up to tonight?!") or if a tough guy show like Crime Story or Hunter was on.

Well it was the eighties then, after all, and Hunter decided to do an episode dealing with AIDS. Dad happened to stop to watch just as on the tv a father handed his son a condom in a bright orange square pack and said "Hey, take this with you." Dad looked at me and asked "What did he just give him?"

I was in a state of crisis. Was Dad really asking? Did he really not know? Should I play dumb and act like I didn't know when I did? Finally I said "I think he just handed him a condom." Hearing me say the word, my poor dad looking like he was having a heart attack. His entire body seemed to seize up, his face contorted in a look of pain, confusion and embarrassment and without one single word, he turned and walked away and did not come back inside for an hour. When he finally did, he paused only long enough to give me a bewildered look and say "I thought it was a Reese's peanut butter cup!!"

My dad had basically three pieces of advice that he imparted daily: Don't do drugs, don't be a whore like your sisters and turn that "nigger shit music" down! To Dad, anything that was not country, was not Johnny Cash, Willie Nelson or Hank Williams, Sr was "nigger music". I never thought to ask him what category this placed Charlie Pride in. He didn't live long enough to encounter Darius Rucker. That guy, no doubt, would have confused him to no end.

A typical conversation with my father went like this:
"What the hell kind of nigger music are you listening to?!"
"Metallica."
"Metallica!? What the hell kind of name is that?! Can they play "Bubbles In My Beer"?!"
"Um...no...I don't think so..."
"They can't play "Bubbles In My Beer"?! Well what the hell good are they?!"

I swear to god I was 29 years old before I realized that Bubbles In My Beer was actually the signature song of Bob Wills and the Texas Playboys and not just something Dad made up to tease me about.

Speaking of Bob Wills, another thing I will never forget about my dad was the death of Hoyle NIx. Hoyle Nix was a fiddle player and western swing band leader in our home town. From what I understood he carried on the legacy of Bob Wills in fine style. I have no idea if my father knew him personally but he took his passing, in 1985, quite hard. He insisted I go with him to the viewing though I didn't know Hoyle Nix from the man in the moon.

You almost could not get into the funeral home for all the flowers. That's what I remember, the flowers that we had to wade through to get up to the casket and the pale, large man inside. My father put a hand on my shoulder and told me to take a good look, there would never be another like him ever again. At the time I had no idea what he was talking about, but I"m sure for my father it was the end of an era.

Ten years later I would be at a dance at the Stampede dance hall listening to Hoyle Nix's son Jody play when I would meet my friend Bill Fuller who ended up being a friend for life. In a small town, there are small coincidences, the actions of which you will never realize until the end of your life.

My father was larger than life, and I expected his funeral to be just as grand of an occasion as that of Hoyle Nix. He may never have played an instrument but he certainly seemed to know everyone in town. It wasn't. It wasn't even close. Almost no one came, but I will get to that in a bit.

As you'll see in reading, musical and movie references rule my life and always have. I can hear a song and remember exactly what was happening the first or last time I heard it, what I was wearing, where I was, how old, everything. For reference I'm chronicling each musical era in my life by correlating it to what was going on, for this is how I remember things best.

The soundtrack to my father's death was Queensryches' Rage For Order and The Warning. I do not remember how exactly I even came to listen to them, I just associate them with a girl named Jamie Kimpton who was my pen pal at the time. Queensryche was the first "music with a message" band I had ever heard. Instead of the usual hair band fare, they staged metal operas and talked about overthrowing political systems. It opened my mind to a lot that I would have never thought of at that young age. When I hear Rage For Order, I still feel the chill of the December when he died. I sat in many backseats of sisters or friends, driving me to Lubbock and Midland to visit dad in one hospital or another. I sat in the back listening to Queensryche on my Walkman. I cannot hear these albums now without feeling the chill of emptiness and grief.

CHAPTER 3

My sister Toni was pregnant when my dad died. My niece Tori Jo came to this world never knowing my dad as her grandfather. I wrote something for my niece so that she would remember him and so that I would never forget.

MY LETTER TO MY NIECE TORI JO MROTZ
I got to thinking about that photo I posted of your mom kissing dad and you know, thinking back, you weren't in her belly then. I think you were just a hope on the horizon at that point. He lived through that Christmas, by the next December he was too sick to get out of the hospital and we have no pictures from that time because it was so horrible. He died the NEXT year on Dec. 16th so technically those pictures were of his last Christmas, but it was the next December that your mom was pregnant with you.

I remember though your mom was HUGELY pregnant and I was so scared that all the stress she was going through was going to cause her to miscarry.

I remember the day of the funeral it was pretty cold, although not as cold as it usually was for December in West Texas and your mom wasn't wearing a coat but she was wearing an old timey lace shawl she had gotten from our store. I kept thinking she was going to catch cold or something. I remember her asking the priest if we could use his quarters for a private moment to compose ourselves before the service. I would have never thought to ask a priest that in a million years, I wouldn't have thought it was allowed, but he let us. I remember your mom looked so elegant with that shawl. I remember her standing on the steps of the church, shaking hands with people and I was thinking "I'm glad she's the one doing this because if anyone says anything to me I'm going to start crying."

It is so crazy to remember a time when we did not have cell phones but I remember right before I was to leave college for Thanksgiving break, they thought Dad only had a few hours to live. I don't remember where he was, if it was Lubbock or Midland but it was in another town and the hospital called Howard College and the call was transferred to the office of my English professor and her secretary took the call and came to get me out of class and when they called my name I just KNEW what it was for. I got up and I was trying to keep from crying until I could at least get out of the classroom. My professor said "You need to go wait out front, someone is coming to pick you up" and she shoved a handful of quarters in my hand so I could make phone calls from the hospital if I needed to tell anyone else(which again seems so foreign, thinking that NO ONE had cell phones). I got out into the hallway and a few feet from the classroom door and just started sobbing and sure enough there was someone coming down the hall. It turned out to be one of my friends and she sort of steered me into the bathroom until I could calm down.

It turned out Dad would live another two months. When he died I had nothing to wear to the funeral and by that I don't mean I didn't have anything nice, I mean I did not have a dress period in my closet. Angela gave me some money and the only place I could go was Wal Mart because it was the only store in town. It was one week before Christmas and FULL of people. So I am just wandering around in a daze, just in total shock, trying to find anything I could wear that was nice.because. you know, it's Wal Mart and all their clothes SUCK.

There was this guy I had a huge crush on. I actually had a crush on 3 guys at the same time that year and they were all best friends. Their names were Joey, Adam and Louis.

I see Louis, and I have NO idea if he knows my dad has died and I don't want to go up and explain because I know I'm going to start crying and I don't want to make a fool of myself. We were all pretty good friends and we all hung out together and had classes together, that was like the one time in my life I was in with the "in" crowd.

Anyway I see him and all I want to do is go up and throw my arms around him and cry on his shoulder but I can't make a big scene.

WELL…I'm looking at him and I'm trying to sort of just…back away and maybe go hide behind something to where I can watch him some more. I start backing up without looking and I knock over an entire tower of camera film!!! It goes CRASHING DOWN and flying everywhere and Louis looks up and sees me. He runs over and grabs me and hugs me and then he kisses my hand and tells me how sorry he is. He and Adam end up going to the graveside services and standing beside me when Dad is buried.

I never forgot him kissing my hand.

I only remember two things about the funeral: It was SO small. Dad knew SO many people and like NO ONE showed up, which really upset me. But he had this one friend named Earnest. Earnest was a good friend to dad, he was nice to me and he seemed like an OK guy but he was also a member of a motorcycle gang and he was a scary looking man. I mean if you saw this guy coming toward you on the street you'd move pretty fast to get to the other side.

So we're sitting in the church and all of a sudden I hear someone just SOBBING at the top of their lungs, like really, really crying. And I'm looking around and all of the family members are around me and I'm thinking "WHO is that and WHY are they carrying on like that?!" Like I felt if anyone needed to be crying like that it was US because we were the ones that really loved Dad and anyone else was just doing it for attention. Finally I looked back to see who was crying so loud and it was Earnest the biker. I never forgot that, EVER.

CHAPTER 4

Somehow in those days and the ones long before, a work ethic was instilled in me that never left. I was not aware of this at the time and would not be until later. With one horrible time of unemployment, when I was dumb enough to leave a cushy, yet insanity producing job in retail management to pursue a teaching career, from the time I was thirteen years old, I always had a job. It has never occurred to me not to work. If I have more than a few days off I feel guilty. Being only marginally employed for a period of a year when I was working for a temp agency and unsure of where the next job or meal was coming from, was one of the closest things to a living hell I have ever experienced.

Having spent most of my life in one classroom or another, I was sure my profusion of education would assure me any job I was qualified for. I was a naive fool and I'm sure, had my father been alive he would have told me as such. My father had nothing against education, but had everything against wasting his hard earned money. Not positive education would do much for me, he agreed to pay for exactly six college hours per semester. That way I could not snivel and complain that he was robbing me of my one chance at a real education, and if for some reason I couldn't cut it, and had to drop out, he wouldn't be out of much money. Looking back I couldn't blame his practicality.

After he died, the two things I felt I was denied, tattoos and higher learning, I chased like Tiger Woods chased white women that weren't his wife. No one was going to stop me from getting either and both required money. The first job I remember having after my dad died was at a grocery chain that declared WE ARE THE BEEF PEOPLE on the side of their store. It sort of sounds like something from the Island of Doctor Moreau, no? I remember two things about that job: the little old ladies who came in and could barely afford what they bought, even though they bought next to nothing. They would stand in line shaking and counting their pennies to buy what couldn't possibly sustain them for the week and even then they would never have enough though, and would have to put things back. All I wanted was to be able to buy groceries for all of them or to at least have a spare fiver to pull out of my pocket and throw in for their bill. The second thing that stood out was my immediate supervisor was a woman who came to work, and worked her shift in a full length fur coat. I'm not sure what she was proving as the only customers we seemed to have were the old women who probably lived on dog food, but she was out to rub it in to someone. She screamed at me once in front of an entire line of customers, why I can't remember. I started crying and was so embarrassed I quit and never came back.

My second job was at McDonalds. I lasted there three days. The third day I was issued two extra uniforms for work and was not allowed to leave for the thirty seconds it would have taken to go lock them in my truck so I stuck them under my register. At the end of my shift I went to get them and they had been stolen. When I told my manager what had happened and asked for another set I was told tough shit and if I wanted another set of uniforms I could pay $30. I declined, the offer and the job.

My next job was actually quite blissful while it lasted. I was a night stocker at a Wal Mart. Working at Wal Mart surely would conjure up visions of hell on earth and it is probably like that for most employees. However, we were lucky: our store, at the time was only open 8 am to 10 pm. I would come in at ten o'clock at night, unload and put up the trucks of stock that came in nightly and would get off work at 7 am, just as the sun was rising. For this I was paid very well. I can't remember what the wage was but I know that it was the best I had gotten paid until then. It was a guaranteed forty hours a week, I had fun coworkers and we never once had to deal with a customer. It was heaven on earth.

It was in that very Wal Mart, working with a bunch of crazy people who had the run of the place that I made one of the greatest musical discoveries of the first few years of my life. We worked with this guy whose real name escapes me but I'll never forget his nickname: Ol'

Roy. He was so named because he bragged that he liked to eat the Wal Mart brand dog food of the same name. One night Ol' Roy brought a tape to play over the PA system for us all to stock by. This was one of the many perks of having an entire store to yourself for ten hours.

As I was putting up some cheap trinket made for 30 cents of sweat shop labor and sold for $5.95, I heard the strangest, most otherworldly melody coming from the speakers. It sounded like Jim Morrison, if Jim Morrison was still alive and singing bluesy heavy metal. I ran up to Ol' Roy and demanded to know who we were listening to.

"Haven't you ever heard Danzig?!" He asked, giving me a funny look. Little did I know the next musical era in my life was about to begin.

No, I had not, but that would not be a problem as Danzig would be the main band I listened to for the next ten years. Wal Mart gave me this and gave me one other thing. One payday I realized I had all my bills up to date and the entire paycheck (what amount this windfall was escapes me but I was a 21 year old living with no rent and only food and a truck payment, so any amount could have been great) to spend on whatever I wanted. I called my best friend Margo and told her we were taking a trip to the big city of Midland to go to a real mall to go shopping. We ate lunch at Red Lobster and then went to Spencer's Gifts and bought a bunch of junk: Metallica t-shirts, a book on Guns N' Roses (I got one copy for myself and another for my niece LeAnn who at the time was my other best friend) and more crap than I can now even remember. It was a great day to be sure but the memory is that much sweeter now, Margo having been killed three years later, a month before her own twenty first birthday. A few years back I got a strange thing in the mail, a color photo copy of the first page of the GNR photo book with the inscription I had given to my niece. She had found it buried somewhere in her things and made a copy of the inscription to send to me. A few months after that she would become a born again Christian and decide that, after all the years we spent as family and best friends, I was a bad influence, a heathen and not the type of person she wanted to associate with. Still, thanks to that job at Wal Mart I still have wonderful memories of that weekend and the two people that are no longer in my life.

My job at Wal Mart lasted about nine months. My Danzig phase lasted ten years and would have lasted longer than that if Danzig 5 hadn't been such an abomination of fake industrial metal shite.

CHAPTER 5

All good things come to an end and so did my blissful nocturnal existence at Wal Mart. The store got converted to a twenty four hour a day location. I was switched to days, which I could not work because of going to college. I quit in order to pursue higher education but considering where it got me, I should have stayed. I should have stayed in a lot of places when my impulse control (or lack thereof) got the better of me. I could have stayed in West Texas and been head manager of Wal Mart but fate had other plans. However, whenever I hear "She Rides" I still feel the urge to pick up a pricing gun.

It took several tries at Math before I graduated. I had just dropped Statistics for a second time when the change over at Wally World occurred. As good as I thought I was, I could not work all night, then turn around with no sleep and go in and be cognizant enough to comprehend Math.

Of course the instant I dropped the early morning class I couldn't keep up with because of work, I had to quit the job and dropped the class for nothing. For the record though, the third time I took Statistics and stayed in the course for more than three weeks, I got the one and only B I have ever received in a Math class in my life.

CHAPTER 6

The only soundtrack I recall for working all day and sleeping all night was Danzig and the good old, bland metal that KBAT used to play from their little station in Odessa that is no longer in existence. After I finally beat down my Math demons, yet found myself unemployed once again, I accepted a job that would change my life. I went into show business. Sort of. In a small town a movie theater is a big deal, it is the closest thing to feeling in sync with the rest of the world that you can get in a town of seventeen thousand. I've always loved watching movies, sharing the experience of joy, surprise, outrage and hilarity with an auditorium of friends and strangers is one of the great rituals of our society. I felt very lucky to be offered a job that involved bringing this ritual to life.

During my time at the movie theater I met the man I would one day marry, I saw two friends buried, I left home for the first time, I put myself through college and earned my Bachelor's degree and I married the man that I met at that little four screen theater in what passed for a shopping mall in West Texas.

Tennessee Williams once wrote "I have come to rely on the kindness of strangers." In my case I have come to rely on the kindness of friends who eventually became strangers. One such friend took pity on me and hired me as a concession girl. Wearing a day glo orange vinyl bow tie and apron I popped popcorn and sometimes sold tickets if it was called for. The ticket booth was a tiny room, painted a deep green with a huge painting of Bette Davis done entirely in black, white, red and green. Some customers thought it was garish but I loved being in that little booth, sealed off from the rest of the world, listening to people call "Driving Miss Daisy" Driving Miss Piggy or calling "Event Horizon" Event Horizontal, or not asking for a ticket for "Crimson Tide", but for its tag line: Danger Runs Deep.

The pay was horrible, barely a step above being a waitress. However, the staff was nice, the hours were easy if near nonexistent, which allowed me plenty of time for college and driving to Dallas on the weekend to go to the occasional punk or metal show or just to leave flowers on Stevie Ray Vaughan's grave, and the work was not hard. I also got a crash course in human nature.

Through this job I learned that not only could people not communicate the name of the movie they were there to see when it was clearly spelled out on the marquee above them, they also could not pronounce the names of the candies we sold. Whoppers, Sour Patch Kids, Milk Duds, all became mangled so horribly, sometimes I would just have them point. I came to realize that cowboys would only order Dr. Pepper. Never did I once see a cowboy order a Coke or a Sprite. I also learned the rules of rationalization: it's okay to buy a large popcorn with butter, a box of Junior Mints and a hot dog if the meal was accompanied by a Diet Coke. Somehow that diet soda, in the mind of every corpulent customer, just cancelled out the other five billion calories they were consuming.

Being friendly with the management meant I got the time off I wanted to go to shows. This was the whole reason I was working: if it came down to either eating or going to a show, I would choose the music. I could buy bologna stock up on re-fried beans and tortillas and subsist on that for the rest of the month, spending the bulk of my pay on driving the five hours to Dallas.

The music I remember most of that time was the Cranberries and Nine Inch Nails.

I saw NiN for the first time when I was 23. I led a very sheltered life thanks to being the only child my mom and dad had together and of the whole pack of kids from other marriages, the youngest. All my sisters were just whores, no way around that so my dad barely let me out of the house.

He died when I was 20 and I just went wild, not with sex and not too much with drinking but I went to every single show I could no matter where it was. If I had to choose between eating for a week and going to a show, I'd go to a show.

I drove by myself, all the way across the state in the dead of winter to see NiN in Dallas at some little place that usually held hockey games. I got there five hours early and stood in sub freezing temps to get a place in line. I had never seen a crowd like that in my life: kids from vampire covens, S&M couples on leashes, every sort of hardcore, heavy metal and punk kid imaginable.

It was The Melvins, the Jim Rose Circus and NiN. The crowd was fucking nuts. The Melvins got booed off the stage even though they were incredible. The crowd went so wild they ripped off the flooring that was kept over the hockey rink bottom to throw at the band. When that didn't work, shit was lit on fire and hurled at the stage. Trent had to come out and tell everyone to knock it off or his band wouldn't play.

I was so young and so naive and so just…convinced I was invincible. I got up to the front and right before NiN goes on, this guy starts flirting with me. He is HOT. I never thought of myself as being good looking or anything and back home guys never gave me the time of day so this was just mind blowing to me. We barely say hello before the lights go down.

Trent takes the stage and his guy wraps his arms around me from behind. For the next two hours we basically have sex right in the second row with our clothes on. It was like having Trent play a private concert in my bedroom. The bad thing was, I didn't exactly SEE the concert as I was twisted around with this dude's hands and tongue all over me but everyone once in a while I'd open my eyes and look up and there was Trent, RIGHT THERE.

I never got the guy's name. When the show was over I was ready to just follow him home, but it turned out we were both from opposite ends of the state and both having to drive back, neither with the means of renting a motel room for the night so we said goodbye there. I lost my coat in the melee and walked out into the snow not feeling a damn thing.

I ended up seeing them again about four years ago with my husband here in town and it was just as cold, but nothing in my life has ever come close to that experience of that first NiN show in Dallas.

I remember that because the last song before the encore was Something I Can Never Have and he sang it in my ear between kisses.

This was hardly the only adventure I experienced at the theater. We had to stop people from engaging in sex while watching Mr Magoo (of all things), we were held personally responsible for the content of the movies we showed and every time a new R rated flick came out, some old lady was telling us we were going to hell.

I have very fond memories of working at the little four screen theater back home. I started out as a concession worker, wearing the hideous neon green and pink vinyl bow tie and apron. We had a lot of fun there, went to parties after work, I could not say I was best friends with anyone there but I certainly had pals. I have a fond memory of being sent to get food with a coworker named Jennifer, a smart assed blond that took no crap from no one. The day was warm and the Cranberries were on the stereo so Jennifer decided we did not need to be back at work any time soon with our coworkers' meals. We drove around town with "Linger" on repeat, her car smelling faintly of pot mixed with Poison perfume.

Jennifer and I were promoted to assistant manager trainees at about the same time. This was a wonderful thing because I got to dump the horrid neon colored. plastic apron and bow tie accessorized, uniform and buy my very first business suit. I will never forget it, a hounds-tooth patterned miniskirt with matching jacket. I felt so much confidence wearing it that for the first time I had the guts to finally speak too this cute guy who frequented the arcade across from the movie theater where I also worked part time. I had actually talked to him once before, when, in an attempt to get him and his friend out so I could close the store on time, I started shutting off breakers, hoping the lack of light would give them a hint. Instead I accidentally turned off the Dungeons and Dragons game they had been battling on heatedly. It got his attention all right, but me in a mini skirt did the job a bit better.

We ended up talking so long I had to shoo him away, afraid I would get fired my first night as assistant for slacking. He didn't seem very happy to leave but at the end of my shift he came back with roses. I married that man. Sixteen years later we are still together and it all happened that the crummy little four screen in what passed for a man in West Texas.

Jennifer, the other assistant trainee, would play a key role in saving my job when things went sour, but that wouldn't be for quite a while.

Not all my memories of the theater were good ones. During my tenure there I buried two of my best friends. The first was my friend Shannon who died on World AIDS Day after a very long, horrible battle with cancer. I had lost my dad maybe two years before to prostate cancer and even though I knew Shannon was suffering, I could not bring myself to go and visit. I called her and we sent letters back and forth, but having spent two years watching my dad waste away into a walking corpse, I could not bear to do the same thing all over again. In my mind I was in denial, sure that she was going to beat it until the night I came home after attending an AIDS rally in Odessa to a ringing phone. It was my friend Amy Williamson telling me Shannon had died.

We received the town newspaper at the movie theater so we could confirm that the movie times printed every day were correct. I was there when the paper arrived with Shannon's obituary in it. I could have ignored it but something wouldn't let me. I opened it and read it and then spent the rest of my shift in the back room sobbing, coming out and composing myself whenever I heard a customer approaching.

I was working at the theater the night my niece called to tell me my brother in law had committed suicide. The manager demanded to know why I was getting a personal call at work, I looked at her and said "My brother in law just killed himself." She said "Go home!" and I did.

I was working at both the theater and at the arcade next door when the single worst even of my life, or at least of my life so far, came hurdling into my life like a runaway train.

CHAPTER 7

I met my friend Margo Glickman through our mutual friend, Rose Saenz. For the longest time I had heard about her but we actually met the night Rose and I went to go see the chamber orchestra play back home in Big Spring. For a town of 17,000 this was a big thing and we got the tickets free through the junior college we were attending. I'll never forget that night for many reasons. It was the first time I met Margo, who was such a teeny tiny thing and not at all what I was expecting, it was the first and only time my father ever told me I was pretty, and at the end of the night, returning home, Margo somehow managed to run her little Ford Escort wagon sideways onto the steps of my dad's store. This I thought would ensure that my dad would forbid me from ever seeing her but dad was oddly casual and helped her steer down from the incline. He would die from cancer about five months later and Margo would sit with me at the funeral barely knowing me at that point. I never forgot that about her.

We crammed more adventures into the short few years we knew each other than many people can claim in a lifetime. We broke more traffic laws, drove drunk way too many times, did more impetuous stupid shit, like stealing street signs and inviting in guys who followed us home to party with us, that we really should have died many times over. It was a great shock when she died and left me behind.

It was the same summer my brother in law killed himself, high on drugs and not thinking clearly, sure he was going back to jail. My sister, his wife went over the deep end and had to be put in the local mental hospital, my niece, the oldest of the family and a hard partyer herself came home to the carnage and had to be the one to clean up the bloody aftermath.

Margo had it made, in my eyes. She had gotten out of our one horse town and her dad was paying for her to attend Texas Tech. He supported her fully, she didn't have to work, all she had to do was study. Lubbock being a dry county, I was constantly driving over to bring her alcohol or she was coming home to party at my place. When we were really brave we partied at her dad's house. This was dicey because her dad had no idea she drank. I remember very clearly popping the cork on a bottle of champagne during a Dallas Cowboy Super Bowl victory (oh where have THOSE days gone?) and Margo freaking out because some of it fizzed out on her dad's carpet.

It was at her dad's record store that bought my first Charlie Sexton and Will Sexton albums and Margo would drive with me to Stevie Ray Vaughan's grave. She was the only person I knew that loved music as much as I did. Together we went to concerts for Alan Jackson, Little Texas and Tracy Lawrence.

While at Texas Tech, Margo met a man who was about 18 years older than her. I honestly don't remember his name, I think I have blocked it all out. Margo had never had a boyfriend or had a guy pay attention to her. This man swept her off her feet. He had no prospects, he was not good looking, he was overweight and wore glasses. He worked as a security guard and had no real savings or prospects to give her any better of a life than she'd had with her father. For whatever reason, she loved him. She dropped out of school, moved in with him, took a job as a night clerk at his parent's motel and when she lost her virginity to him, she became pregnant. As her friends, we thought she was nuts and I know her father did not approve, nor did her mother who lived in Dallas. Still, Margo seemed completely happy and they were married in May of 1995 in a thrown together ceremony at the local Days Inn when Margo was 7 months pregnant.

It all came to an end on July 4, 1995 when my phone rang at 4 am. Under normal circumstances I was usually very friendly on the phone, even the middle of the night wrong number, figuring an honest mistake didn't deserve sniping. However that summer I was working two jobs and taking summer classes at the University of Texas of the Permian

Basin, sixty miles away in Odessa. Sleep was rare as gold to me. That night I said a surly hello and when the voice on the other end of the line identified herself as Margo's aunt, I just said "Okay, what can I do for you?"

Then came the dialog that I know by heart because it has played in my head for the last 15 years.

"Margo went into labor tonight."
"She did? Well…you could have waited to call until later on…what did she have?"
"Joey…Margo's dead."
"…what?! What happened?"
"We don't know."
"And the baby?!"
"He's dead too. "
" Oh my god…is this…? Am I having a nightmare?"
"Oh my child, I wish you were."

I slid down to sit on the floor, suddenly empty, like a building gutted by fire and only appearing to be still a structure on the outside. Desperate to hear a friendly voice, I called my niece who was a mutual friend of Margo's and the same age. My niece however was experimenting with acid and was completely incoherent to speak to. I then sat there until the sun came up, fearing if I did fall back asleep I really would think it was all a dream and then what was I to do? Call Margo's father and say "Hey, did your daughter really die last night or did I dream it?"

At nine am I had to call all of our friends and tell them the most horrifying news anyone could think of. It would turn out that the doctor was not present in the delivery and the anesthesiologist working that night was high on drugs that he had been stealing from the hospital. He was so messed up he botched Margo's epidural and that stopped her heart and sent her into seizures. The nurses on duty were not fully certified and they panicked. In the panic they did not think to get the baby out or simply did not get him out in enough time.

I remember going straight from work in my white shirt and black pants and joining Rose and her sister in going to Margo's dad's house to make "the visit", what you were "supposed to do" when someone died: call on the relatives. We all just sat there in the living room staring at each other. The house never felt the same, all the life had gone out of it.

The next day I was fired from my job at the arcade, the owner would tell me that I wasn't working hard enough since my friend's death, I was too distracted and left streaks on the video game screen when I cleaned them with Windex. At any other time I would have been incensed but at that point I didn't care.

We spent four years together and had the time of our lives. We met right before my dad died, and I will never forget, I had maybe known Margo a month and she came and sat RIGHT next to me at my Dad's funeral and held my hand. I will never forget that. From then on we were just inseparable even though she was my niece's age and not mine. We did more cool shit, it seemed, than anyone on earth and with all the drinking and driving and acting stupid we did, we should have died together, and the fact that we didn't, the fact that she died first and I was left here was the worst thing to deal with.

The morning of the funeral we all met at Denny's and I was the first one there. When I hear that song One Headlight, when Jakob Dylan talks about seeing the sun coming up over the funeral at dawn, I just see myself right there at the counter, watching the sun come up through the windows and knowing I was about to have to go bury my best friend. My sister, my niece and her little sister arrived first, then Rose and her sister Bonnie and then the rest of our clique, and we all went together. There was just a graveside service where someone sang a bluegrass version of Amazing Grace that had been featured in the movie Maverick.

When we got to the cemetery, there was this whole OTHER group of girls there, this whole other circle of friends. She had not told us about them, nor apparently, them about us. We just stood there and stared at each other, no one said anything. It was really wild, we had no idea who these girls were. I had been to Tech and met the few friends she had there, and none of them were in the bunch with these other girls. It was very strange.

Margo was buried one year and one month before her twenty first birthday. Not a day goes by that I don't think about her.

I grieved every day for ten years. It still hurts, I feel like I am still in mourning but it is not as bad as it once was. Before I turned straightedge, on the anniversary of her death, I would drink until I was unconscious. I sat at her grave and talked to her as if she was still there. I could not fathom that she had left me. In our twenties death means nothing as we head towards it. I was sure we were going to die, I was sure we were going to die together. The fact that she died and left me behind seemed like cruel and unusual punishment for some sin I had not yet committed.

Her father and mother, who were divorced, would eventually sue the hospital and it would come to light that the anesthesiologist was on drugs, high at the time of Margo's labor, high on drugs he was stealing from the hospital. He killed her, quite simply put. By the time this came to light I as no longer living in Big Spring and I intentionally avoided all updates on the trial. I knew if I ever found out the individuals name, I would drive back to Lubbock, I would hunt him down, and if I couldn't kill him with my bare hands, I would die trying. I wish I could say I came to grips with it. I wish I could say I w as the better man and I forgave him. I didn't and I still feel the same way to this very day. Very few people have understood this and I have always felt the pressure to give it over to God, let it go, whatever but I can't. To this day I will put on Strength of the World by Avenged Sevenfold and dream of making him pay for what he did. One of the many reason I love the man who would become my husband is because he told me he would have done the exact same thing.

The first six months I would run the high school track alone at night, late at night, midnight or two am. I would look longingly at every passing car and think "Take me, kill me, rape me, I don't deserve this life. I'm alone, here in the middle of the night, you know you wanna..." No one ever did, I ran along with Will Sexton's "Their Game" on my Walkman, a forgotten album, by a forgotten songwriter, in a time that will haunt me until the day I die. Remember Walkmans? They recently just stopped production of them. It's a cassette tape player, for those of you too young to remember.

The soundtrack for my mourning is One Headlight by the Wallflowers, Ugly All Day by the Charlie Sexton Sextet, Life By The Drop, by Stevie Ray Vauhan, Gone Away by the Offspring, Strength of the World by Avenged Sevenfold, Bleed Black by AFI and Passing Show by Will Sexton. This is my jukebox of the damned who are doomed to be left behind alone on this earth. Margo found out If the angels looked like Will long before I would. That was the one thing I could not get over, she went first. Sometime within that six months I did the only thing I felt fitting to honor her: I got a tattoo of an angel who looked like Will tattooed on my thigh. The artist, Sheri Baucham was a huge fan of Stevie Ray Vaughan. I took her photos of Will Sexton and she created for me an angel playing an acoustic guitar, with long brown hair, brown eyes and wearing a denim chambray shirt. Whenever anyone asked me who it was or what it was for, I lied. My pain was none of their business.

CHAPTER 8

Things would change dramatically in my life and working environment after Margo's death. Our district manager was called on to open his own sixteen screen theater in Corpus Christi. Our main manager and her assistant, a tall wiry kid nicknamed Twink were asked to come aboard and helped run it. More than anything I wanted to leave West Texas and if I'd had any sense I would have done it long before. By this time I had been moved up to the management trainee program and when I asked, I was invited along. However, I was in the middle of a semester at UT Permian Basin and without the wealthy parents the two managers had, I needed the summer to work to have the money for the move.

The two of them left in April and the theater was taken over by a gaunt man named Mr. Jones who was young, built like a heroin addict and dressed like he was in the mafia. Little did I know his arrival would signal the end of my job at that particular theater.

The plan had been that the main manager, the woman I will talk about later on as "Joey Douglass' sidekick", because she was, and Twink would move to Corpus and myself and my friend Joey Douglass would follow in the Fall. They did just that and got an apartment together. Down deep I knew Joey D would never follow through as she never seemed to follow through with any grand plan she had. She had plenty of grand plans, had our whole life. She was going to be a singer, then an actress, then maybe a record producer or tour manager, or maybe do something in the movies. She was going to move to California to go to college and study acting and the performing arts. She never did anything of these things. She finished high school and went to work renting videos and that was it for that time in our lives. I can't really say anything though because at this point in my life I thought I would be working for Rolling Stone or at the very least the Austin American Statesman, instead of being the most educated person in Nazi Burger World. I'm getting way ahead of myself though. Luckily by the time

I realized she wasn't going, I had met my boyfriend and he was more than willing to come with me.

Apparently the big sixteen screen theater wasn't for everyone. I'm not sure what happened in Corpus Christi but Twink left in the middle of the night without telling anyone and came back to Big Spring with his tail between his legs, leaving the other manager with the rent and a lease on the apartment. He was not the same person he was when he returned. He was no longer the happy prankster I had known from high school. He was surly and vengeful and for whatever reason had decided he was no longer my friend.

Mr Jones was sketchy as a manager at best and when Twink returned, it was clear a new order was forming. Twink had always been a friendly guy, he had attended many parties at my house and I considered him a friend. When he came back he wanted nothing to do with me. When I asked why he didn't stay he told me that Corpus had "too many Mexicans". I said that was ridiculous because our hometown was probably forty percent Hispanic. To this he responded "Yeah, well we have a better class of Mexican here. The Mexicans in Corpus were just dirty. There was a difference." That was the last somewhat civil thing I ever remember him saying to me. After that he only spoke to the other managers, all except me, were male.

On nights that I worked, deposits I was supposed to count went mysteriously missing, sometimes Mr. Jones said he took them home and brought them back the next day, sometimes they were lost for days at a time, where he was probably floating loans out of them.

During one such instance I panicked and asked one of the employees, a girl I had known for many years and considered a good friend to come help me look for the deposit and recount what I had. I'll call her Grendel. It was highly against the rules to have anyone other than a manager in the office with you when you were counting the safe but I trusted Grendel because she had been my best friend for many years, since some time in high school if I recall.

The next day she turned me in to Mr. Jones and told him I had let her in the office. That is when all hell broke loose. A security team from the corporate offices was called in to investigate me, not Mr. Jones, but me. I was threatened with being beaten up by the wife of another assistant manager who also tried to run my boyfriend off the road. The worst, in my mind, was that on a night when only Twink and his new girlfriend were working with me, I set down a library book I was reading on break along with my glasses, that I needed to see, that cost three hundred dollars, that I could not afford to replace. I set it under the counter where the ticket printer was located where only employees would have access to. I left them for maybe two hours while I went to work elsewhere in the theater. When I came back they were gone. I questioned both people but both plead dumb and swore they had no idea where they could have been.

My eyes have always been bad. I was born with congenital cataracts and have had so many surgeries on my eyes I have honestly lost count of them all. The year before all hell was breaking loose at work, while attending UT Permian Basin and working at the theater I suffered a retinal tear so bad, my retina came completely off my eye. I had three surgeries in three months. This happened two months after Margo's death and I suddenly found myself about to have major surgery in the same hospital where she had died. Recovery was slow and unbelievably painful. I had to spend twenty three of twenty four hours face down, in bed, lying flat on my stomach. I could not move my head, I could not get up. I was allowed five minutes out of every hour to use the restroom or eat. Bathing was out of the question. My retina had to be completely reconstructed and made to stay on my eye. There was no way I could care for myself. I subsequently had to have three more, smaller surgeries, one called a "gas-fluid exchange". During this procedure I was wide awake and aware. The only area to be numbed was my eyeball itself. A needle was stuck into the side of my eye to drain out collected fluid as another needle was inserted in the other side of my eye to inject gas into the gas bubble holding my reconstructed retina in place. After these came months and months of having a white hot laser shot directly through my iris to the back of my eye to seal the retina in place, making sure it would never tear again. In those months I experienced more unrelenting, physical pain, trauma and fear, than I ever have in my life.

My parents were dead, one sister was in a mental hospital after the suicide of her husband, the other was married to a drug dealer and lower level gang member. I ended up moving in with my father's first wife, my sister Toni's mom, Jean, who did not hesitate to take me in and take care of me for three months. I quit my job, gave up college for a semester and spent six months in bed recovering, fighting the doctor's prognosis that I would never see out of that eye again.

Everyone at the theater knew I'd had all those surgeries because I had taken nearly six months off work to recover. Knowing this, the manager, the assistant manager or his girlfriend stole the glasses that I needed to see and threw them away. They had cost me three hundred dollars and I did not have the money to replace them. I had to swallow my pride and ask one of my sisters to buy another pair for me, though I would have rather walked on glass than asked for help, especially from someone with such shady dealings.

There is no doubt in my mind those prescription glasses were taken away on purpose just to spite me. I have never had anything so deliberately cruel done to me in my life. I've never forgiven Twink. I run into him on many social networking sites because we graduated from the same school in the same year but I stay away and to this day, years later, I have to force myself not to say something nasty to him.

Grendel never spoke to me again. Several years later when we both found ourselves attending the wedding of my friend Rose as bridesmaids she still refused to speak to me. I think of her a lot as the years roll on because one night we made a drunken pact to meet in Dublin Ireland to celebrate the year 2000. She probably made it there. Who knows.

CHAPTER 9

It has been nearly twenty years now since all these events took place so my memory is fairly fuzzy on some. I cannot recount all of the misdeeds that took place with Twink and Mr. Jones, but I do know at the time I kept a list of everything and brought it with me to the security team interrogation. They called Jennifer, who by this time had moved on to another job. After everything that had happened at that little four screen theater, I had no reason to trust anyone. I had considered every person who worked there my friend and in the end I could trust no one. However Jennifer was the only person who came through for me and told the truth, corroborating all my stories.

I left cleared of all charges and a rush was put on my transfer out of that location. I can't really remember what they did to Twink. I never had to deal directly with him again. However, I do know that when I got home his mother called me and cussed me out for over an hour and told me I was going to hell. I should have hung up but I was so shell shocked, I had been to this lady's house, she had treated me like a daughter. What a big, tough man, stealing my prescription eye glasses and siccing his mother on me.

I was tempted to wish baldness and impotence on Twink but karma caught up with him anyway. The Christmas after I left home, the little four screen was bought out by a private individual who fired the entire staff including Twink, Mr. Jones and my ex best friend. Last I heard of Twink he was working for his dad, selling used cars.

Once I was assured a job waited for me in Corpus Christi it was a great time to be alive. I was young, in love, had a job waiting for me and was leaving my hometown for the very first time.

We spent the next few days telling everyone goodbye. I drove to Odessa and had one last meal with my friend Kay Courtright. I had met Kay at UT Permian Basin and she was old enough to be my mom.

We immediately took to each other. She was recovering from a sudden divorce and was going back to school to get an English degree. We ended up in all the same classes. Together we survived Women in Eighteen Century Literature by decoding the teacher's secret trick of asking about the most obscure character in the novels to make sure we had read them. For example, we never forgot the infamous "Who's Sally?" that ended one particularly brutal quiz. Sally was the illegitimate daughter of the maid. For years to come we would look at each other and say "Who's Sally?" and burst out laughing, no one else getting the joke. She took to calling me "Joseph" instead of Joey and egging her on, when we met new people I would introduce myself as her son and watch the confounded looks of the other people. We didn't care, we were besties just as if we were in sixth grade again. We got each other through insane course work and put together an entire lesson plan on cowboys for a Children's Literature class that somehow led to us meeting western author Elmore Kelton. I still have the book he autographed for me, telling me good luck in my pursuit of a writing career.

Each day I would drive sixty miles to Odessa to attend school and sixty miles back. I loved those drives through the barren flatlands and scrub. They were not chores for me, they were times to dream, reflect and grow. UTPB was the closest university there was and nothing was going to deter me from going. Of course back then gas was barely a dollar a gallon so it wasn't like the drive hurt my pocketbook. The soundtrack for these sojourns was Joe Ely's Love and Danger, The Charlie Sexton Sextet's Wishing Tree and anything by Melissa Etheridge. I hear them now and I see the highway lined with dirt fields and cotton and the endless horizon blurred by dust storms. I miss Interstate 20 like I miss all those who have come and gone from my life.

In leaving West Texas I left what little family I had, lifelong friends, and the only church I had ever belonged to, a small Pentecostal congregation that could never keep a preacher for more than a couple of years before small town boredom and un-Christian like gossip did them all in. Still, the promise of a decent job far away from my hometown was too good to pass up.

My boyfriend and I packed everything that could go, picking through twenty five years of pack rattery, and piled it into my mint green GMC Sonoma sport truck that was pulling a small U-Haul trailer. I was able to take everything except my dog, Sabo.

Dad had chosen to settle us about ten miles outside the city limits on a sprawling piece of land. The main lot had two houses that shared giant front and back yards, surrounded by cinder block and chain link fences. Then there was a shed with room for two cars plus two storage rooms, another two car garage facing the road, a chicken coop, a fire pit, two plowed fields, one on either side of the houses, and about another 7 acres to boot that Dad nostalgically referred to as "The Lightening Sea Range". I have no clue why he called it this. On this massive spread of property dad kept every breed of dog imaginable, ridge-backs, shepherds, setters, chows, labs and every variety of mutt. Along with the dogs we raised chickens, ducks, cats, peacocks, geese and turkeys. The geese and peacocks were my favorite. The peacocks sounded like sirens and were loud as all hell when someone approached and the geese were just plain mean. They would come up behind people and bite their butts, thighs and ankles, whichever they happened to come in contact with first. My nieces were terrified of them.

When dad passed I had to sell off the animals one by one. I just did not have the time and money to care for them all. Sabo, however, was like part of the family. He was half shepherd, half pit bull. I cannot even remember when we got him but I know it had to have been around my sophomore year of high school because I named him after Dave "The Snake" Sabo of the band Skid Row.

Dad always drove a truck and kept several dogs in the back, whether for protection or just to show off, I do not know and never thought to ask. Dad never let me drive his truck, never let me near it unless I was riding in it and me learning to drive was completely out of the question growing up. I was allowed to get my license but once I got it I was never allowed near anything with four wheels, even the junked pieces of crap he took as collateral when he loaned money.

When he died I chose my first new vehicle as a tribute to him, a bright green GMC truck, much like the green trucks of one brand or another he had driven all through my childhood. I also chose a truck specifically so I could take Sabo riding in the back, though by this time he was so old and had arthritis so bad he could no longer take a running leap and clear the closed tailgate like he could when he was a pup. By that time he would walk up, place is paws on the lowered tailgate and patiently wait for me to hoist his hind legs up as well.

Sabo was way, way too old to make the trip to Corpus and having lived his life on a huge stretch of land there was no way we could imprison him in an apartment complex, even though by this time he spent more time indoors than he did out. It was decided he would go to live with our neighbor Pam, who had known me since the day I was born. Pam and her daughter Jeannie lived up the road from us and had a good sized place themselves with dogs and horses and cattle. The night before we left, my boyfriend and I walked there though it was a good ways down the road, it was down in a steep incline and we knew the truck and trailer would never make it up out of there. We took Sabo with us and at first he trotted around happily and surveyed the new digs. That was until Jeannie's dog George (named after George Strait) decided to get friendly with us and come up for a nuzzle. Then here came Sabo running up and snarling and getting between us and George with more energy than we'd seen in years.

The next morning we set out for Corpus Christi, where it almost never got colder than fifty degrees. It was August and unbearably hot. However, that winter, during the first cold snap, Sabo decided he'd had enough and wanted to come home. Unfortunately we were no longer there. Not knowing this, he froze to death on our old back porch, waiting for someone to let him in.

He was the best dog I ever had. Sometimes at night I still dream about him. My song for Sabo is by Neil Young who wrote about a dog that went running after deer and wasn't afraid of jumping off a truck in high gear and was "the best ol hound dog I ever did know.", and Dog Years by Rush, talking about one year is like seven and before you know it you're chasing cars in "doggie heaven". If there is a heaven for dogs, I have no doubt my Sabo is there, riding in the back of an old Ford truck, running from one side of the bed to the other to see which has the best view. My dad is in the driver's seat, blasting country music from the 1980's as they belch smoke up and down the golden streets of paradise.

CHAPTER 10

My hometown of Big Spring, Texas is a good place to be born and a good place to die. It is no place to live for any amount of time. I feel sorry for those who lived there and never left. It is insular and ignorant and racist. Time moves slow there and things never change. You are not allowed to be anything other than a farmer or rancher; you must drink, you must fuck, you must listen to AM country music and play football. If you are not set to do these things from cradle to grave you do not belong there. I never belonged and was never ever so happy to leave anywhere in my life.

I knew absolutely nothing about Corpus Christi, I went there exactly twice before the day we moved, once for the grand opening of the theater and once to scout for apartments. To say I got lucky was an understatement. I had two days off to scout for apartments and the drive alone was eight hours. I went there alone; my boyfriend could not take off from work. Joey Douglass' side kick was supposed to let me stay at her place and for some reason got called out of town herself. I was planning on staying with her and only brought money for gas. With an apartment guide I checked out places to live on two of several major streets that intersected with the freeway that would take me to work. Looking back most of these, especially those closest to the theater were in horrible neighborhoods. I somehow managed to choose the two nicest streets, getting approved for an apartment on the farther of the two from where the new theater was. That night I slept in my truck at a rest stop on the highway. I had done this many times before in going to concerts and I shudder now to think of my utter dumb fearlessness.

I had a job barely making over minimum wage, my boyfriend, having only known me three months, left his job to follow me and had no guarantee of work. The only way I had to money to move was selling both houses and the whole "Lightening Sea Range" to my half sister Toni Jo. Young, in love, feeling invincible, and with a tiny bit of money in our pockets, we were ready to hit the road,

Texas can feel like a country unto itself, it is simply that huge. It took us two days to drive from Big Spring to Corpus Christi, a slow haul with my 5 speed manual transmission, bed full of possessions and U Haul full to the top with more. We told our friends and relatives goodbye, spent the night in a house with no gas for the stove and set out at a decent hour. I wish I could tell you the 1996 soundtrack we listened to on the way, but the only band that sticks in my mind is Everclear. I just remember it as long and exhausting, full of slow chugging treks up winding hills around Kerrville.

We arrived in Corpus in the middle of the pink water debacle. Corpus has had ongoing problems with its water supply, so bad at one point that the entire city came to a standstill when all water was ruled contaminated with fecal matter and everyone had to boil their water or use bottled. That summer so much chlorine was in the water supply that it turned the water in some places pink. The water in our apartment complex wasn't pink but it tasted exactly like swallowing swimming pool water. But having the pickup still hooked to a trailer and no way to just zip on over to a convenience store or grocery store, with temperatures in the high nineties, we had no choice but to drink down the nasty water or die of thirst as we unloaded all our belongings ourselves.

It was quite a change going from West Texas to South Texas. The first thing I noticed was the proliferation of palm trees. I had never seen so many palm trees before, it reminded me of California and made the surroundings seem even more surreal. All the girls were beautiful, stunningly so. They all looked like Mexican soap stars. All the men were short and everyone had tattoos. I had always been shunned at home for having (at the time) ten tattoos—I have since lost count of mine at twenty five. No one looked at me strange, no one made rude comments like they did back home, nd no one insulted me or asked if I was a lesbian or a gang member. A professor at A & M summed it up so well for me and said something I never forgot. She had complimented me on my tattoos and I remember saying "Where I came from, girls who had tattoos were looked down on." She replied "Where you came from, I bet girls who thought for themselves were looked down on too." I never forgot that. Lastly, the biggest difference between South and West Texas, while the girls may have been beautiful, they all got pregnant when they were thirteen and not only was it socially acceptable, it was pretty much expected and no one questioned it or complained or tried to fix the problem.

=+=

It was new and terrifying to be working at a freshly built sixteen screen movie theater, the first in the area to feature stadium seating. This was the big leagues. The place was huge; the lobby looked like a ballroom complete with black and white squared flooring that reached for miles it seemed. The giant marquee full of three hundred light bulbs and pin striped in neon could be seen from the highway and lit up the night like a carnival.

Our management staff was wildly diverse and would end up being a revolving door of managers coming and going. We worked long hours, running up and down every inch of the giant theater keeping everything running steady. Like any large staff there was unscrupulous goings on. A hot young female manager snagged an older manager away from his wife and child; our general manager had several reported liaisons with several female assistants and ended up stealing the wife away from game room manager. Did I mention the general manager looked exactly like Eugene Levy? He did. But he was also the manager of the hottest new place in town and that had to have held some appeal. The employees he was linked to quickly moved up the ranks and got raises. I couldn't stand the man within the first two weeks of working with him. I received one raise in five years.

As soon as I settled in to the theater I also jumped right back into school, enrolling at Texas A & M Corpus Christi. UT Permian Basin, when I attended, had existed entirely in a three story building with a cafeteria next door. I got spoiled to having all my classes in one place. Texas A & M Corpus Christi was way out on the water, twenty minutes by car and an hour by public transportation. It was huge and rambling and once you were there, you stayed because it just too far to get to anywhere if you wanted to leave. So on the days I had an hour or two between classes I was forced to stay on campus. It probably did amazing things for my study habits which was good because A & M required a semester of art and two semesters of Spanish in order to graduate.

The schedule at work could be grueling at times. When I was in the concession department, every Thursday night we had to do inventory, counting every single cup, bag of popcorn, box of Sweet Tarts and every pickle in every open pickle bucket. This routinely kept us out until three in the morning. The first time I was out that late I was driving home when I met my boyfriend who was walking toward the theater, though the theater was at least 17 miles away. He had gotten so worried when I hadn't come home on time he had set out to try and find me, god love him. Our boss, being particularly masochistic, made the schedules so that whoever closed one night would open the next morning. At the time my boyfriend was working as a stock clerk at Sears and had to be at work at six am. I would work until 3 am, go home, sleep until five, take him to work, go back home and sleep and be back at work at nine in the morning.

=+=

Two months after moving to Corpus, during the premiere of the twentieth anniversary edition of Star Wars I left the theater at three in the morning to find an empty space where I had parked my truck. Someone stole it out of the parking lot, drove it until it ran out of gas, eighty miles away and ditched it. When I told my boss this, without showing a hint of sympathy, he turned to some sycophant that was being shown around and said "Poor girl, she came from a tiny town.

She's in the big city now, huh?", and walked away. Thanks Jerk, your lack of security and lighting played no part in it at all!

I loved that truck, I got it back and it ended up lasting me eleven years, longer than the job at the theater.

I stayed with the theater nearly seven years. I stuck it out, year in and year out, working every holiday and not spending one single one with my boyfriend for seven years. I stayed through not having a raise, watching the revolving door of managers spin around, I missed one day in seven years and that was it. My boss grudgingly let me off the night I received my Bachelor of Arts degree from A & M but forced me to attend a mandatory staff meeting the next morning at seven am. He also let me off on February fourteenth, nineteen ninety nine in order to get married to my boyfriend. We had no money for a honeymoon but it didn't matter, he wouldn't have let me off anyway.

He was the single most spineless man I've ever met. Rather than kicking out idiots who brought their crying toddlers to rated R films that were sure to give the poor kids nightmares anyway, he would give them free passes and invite them back. Yeah sure, come annoy the hell out of the other paying customers who popped for a baby sitter some other night.

The customers were no smarter in South Texas than they were in West Texas. If we had a row of seven registers and six were manned, they would inevitably go and stand at the one empty register and expect to be helped. They would stand in front of the popcorn popper, watching the newly popped kernels overflowing from the kettle and ask "Is that popcorn fresh?" Almost every single night after the concession was shut down, the lights turned off, the popcorn popper, nacho warmer, and pickle bucket emptied out and all registers turned off, without fail customers would come and ask the janitorial staff to sell them popcorn or candy.

Things broke down and they were either duct taped together or just ignored. For example we had one projector that had a short circuit in it. Whenever the film being fed through it hit a certain point it tripped a switch that flipped the regular soundtrack to digital. Most of the time, this was not a problem. However when we debuted Saving Private Ryan, the print had an English soundtrack and a French digital soundtrack. Did my boss send it back? No. Did he pay extra to get someone to come in right away and fix the projector? No. Did he put it on another projector? No, that would have required common sense. He put it on the broken one and then told the projectionist, who was busy with fifteen other projectors:

"Stand here and watch it and when it flips over to French, flip it back to English."

Well of course this just had your worst nightmare written all over it. And when the projectionist was called away or forgot and the crowds began to riot because American World War II soldiers were speaking French, he hid in his office and let me to deal with them.

I was so sure that once I got my Bachelor's degree things would change, I would get a raise, I would get respect, but nothing did. My boss continued to sleep his way through the company and I continued to get the shaft despite glowing evaluations.

While at the theater, dad's first wife, my sister Toni's mom, the woman who took care of me when I had no one else, Jean, had a stroke and died. I was not allowed off to go home for the funeral. My husband's younger brother died a week after we moved to Corpus and I took the job. I was allowed one day off to drive him home and leave him. I had to wait a week until my next day off to drive back and pick him up, a week later.

It was not all doom and gloom at the theater. I was trained to manage all aspects of the theater, concession, box office, ushering, projection. I was in charge of counting vast sums of money and never had a shortage on my watch. I hired, recruited and trained employees and even made two lifelong friends. John Fanning was then a chubby kid I hired for the usher department. He has since become our wrestling pay per view buddy and the one person I know to call when no one else could help me out. We have now known each other for close to fourteen years and he has become very close to family. I also met Lance Carter who worked in the game room (though not the guy whose wife was swept off her feet by our Eugene Levy look alike boss). He left the theater right after I did and we ended up working in the same place, but I will get to that later.

CHAPTER 11

I participated in my first Rocky Horror picture show as a presenter. It took twenty garbage bags full of trash to haul it all out and we did not get off work and get done until about four in the morning. We did fun promotions for movies like Mulan, for which we received an award from Disney and The Crow City of Angels. I met some great kids and gained invaluable experience in how to deal with customers because out of any place I'd ever worked, the theater had the rudest customers with which I've ever dealt.

On December of 1997, while still at the theater and living on a budget, my husband and I indulged in a trip to the Texas State Aquarium. It was a very warm December that year and I remember I was wearing a black sleeveless dress that laced up the back that I had bought from Victoria's Secret on close out. We were at the otter tanks when my boyfriend quipped "You otter know I love you!" and kissed me. We have always shared a very goofy, pun oriented sense of humor. After this he led me out on to the beach where I could see dark storm clouds building on the horizon of the surf and could feel the wind starting to cool. He started reminiscing about all we had been through at that point, a mere two years together that seems like a drop in the bucket now. Before I knew it he had dropped down to one knee and was proposing. Of course I said yes, I didn't even have to think. We drove back home and found a Christmas card from the manager that hired me at the four screen years before. Her mom sent us thirty dollars as a Christmas present. What a coup considering we had no money at that time. We gratefully took it and went out for a celebratory dinner at Ruby Tuesdays restaurant. Ruby Tuesdays would end up being closed down, when my husband and I hit a rough patch the theater manager (Joey Douglass' sidekick, you'll read about her later.) would demand I divorce him. At the time she gave me this advice, she had never been married herself and to my knowledge, had never even been in a long term relationship. When I refused she and her family disowned me pretty much. She moved on from the theater long before I did and when I left. Even though she hired me, knew first hand that I had only called in sick twice in seven years and had worked side by side with me for most of those seven, knowing the iron clad work ethic I had, she refused to be put down as a reference or write me a letter of recommendation when I left as well. All because I chose to honor the vow of "til death do us part."

So there I was, newly married and with a Bachelor's degree, barely getting paid over minimum wage to do all the things regular mangers got full wage and benefits for. But hey, I got all the free popcorn I could eat!

Still, free movies and popcorn will only get you so far. In order to become a full assistant manager and receive benefits, insurance, vacation time, and the like, a trainee had to take and pass a practicum. You got a little booklet with all the criteria in it, you had to master each department, be tested in it, and at the end you would go to another theater and run it for a day all by yourself. My packet was finished. All I needed to do was get my managers approval to take the test. Each time I asked he simply said "You're not ready.", just like every time I got evaluated, even though I got all eights and nines out of a possible ten, he would say "You're doing so well, but there's no money in my budget for a raise right now." Then he'd treat himself to elaborate off shore fishing trips with the bonuses he earned by cutting his budget and his staff, running the theater on a skeleton crew and never paying anyone what they were worth unless they were sleeping with him. I was so sure things would change after earning my Bachelor's degree but he could have cared less.

My husband and I have always had a very odd sense of luck. We've never won any large sum of money but we are lucky in very peculiar things. For example, every time the rockabilly/western swing band, The Derailers, came to town, I always won tickets from the local country station, KFTX. I won so much that when the lead singer left the band, my husband swore it was because I had bankrupted them by winning so often. I'll write much more about the Derailers later on. They definitely defined an era of music for me.

Getting back to our vows...We planned for a wedding back home in the church I came of age in, but had no idea how I'd get the time off for it or how we'd pay for it with neither of us having our parents around. We didn't decide on a date right off but we knew we didn't want something cheesy like Valentine's Day to be our anniversary. Fate had other ideas.

There was a brand new radio station in town that winter called THE BEACH 96.5 that played pop music. To introduce themselves they had a contest where they would marry twenty five couples simultaneously on Valentine's Day in Heritage Park, a park built around completely restored turn of the century houses. All you had to do was write an essay on why you should win. I've always believed the one thing I knew how to do well was communicate in print. So I entered. Low and behold I came home one day from work to find a message on my answering machine (remember those? Land lines and answering machines?) announcing that I had won and to call the radio station back.

I was so excited when I gave them my boyfriend's name I misspelled it.

We won the ceremony, the reception, local hotel stay, the garter, the photos, a manicure for both bride and groom and a hair style for the bride, the license and the grooms tux. All we had to provide were the rings and the dress. My friend PJ couldn't come down from Philadelphia for the ceremony so she bought me a beautiful gown. We got the rings on credit and we were good to go. The only two people to show up from my side of the family I no longer speak to, but Axl Rosebush's mom and her boyfriend of the moment came down, one of my sisters took photos and it was an all-around excellent experience. It is very strange not having close family. I had no one to help me get ready. I opened the door to my apartment at seven am on February fourteenth, trying to figure out how to get my train down two flights of apartment stairs and wondering how me, my dress and my groom would fit in my little 1990 GMC Sonoma sport truck. It was surreal and wonderful and I never forgot it.

I was also lucky enough to get the day off from work!

CHAPTER 12

In September of 1999 I realized finally that things were never going to get better. I began to actively look for another job and was immediately hired at a place called Kirkland's in the better of the two malls as an assistant manager. That job was a disaster from day one. When I interviewed I was asked if I knew anything about interior design. I said no. I was hired anyway. I should have known how the rest of the job would go when I showed up for work my first day. I was supposed to attend a staff meeting on Sunday. The general manager did not tell me that on Sunday the front mall doors did not open until noon. The meeting was at nine am. I had no idea how to get in and the general manager did not bother to inform me. I had to go around the mall, trying every door until somehow someone took pity on me and showed me where the back entrance of Kirklands' was and how to ring the bell to get them to open the door. Rather than saying "Oh I'm sorry for not telling you how to get in." I was yelled at for being late.

At Kirkland's I got the distinct impression that they hired me because they thought I was Hispanic. I was the only non-Hispanic working there and they asked me point blank why I couldn't speak Spanish. I replied "Because I'm not Mexican, I'm Arab." When they found out I wasn't, they hated my guts and did everything they could to make my job a living hell.

From then on it was just one horrible experience after another. On the days I was slated to open by myself, three quarters of the staff would call in. I was dumb enough to give a two weeks' notice to the theater so I was working both jobs pulling 12-15 hour shifts every single day. I was issued a key to the store and the night before I was supposed to open, another assistant asked to borrow it, claiming she had left hers at home. Like an idiot I let her and then she conveniently "forgot" to give it back to me. Working twelve hours every day I as exhausted to the point that my memory would just black out. I didn't think to get the key back, in fact I was so intent on going home and going to bed

I forgot about the whole thing until I got up to open the store the next morning. Of course I didn't know the last name of the skank that took my key on purpose. I had no way of getting into the store. I ended up having to call security and have them call the GM who lived forty five miles away to have her come and open the store for me. I was written up for "Losing" my key. Nothing happened to the other assistant who "borrowed" it.

The whole point of Kirkland was to stuff as much shit into one tiny store as you could. In order to do this you had to get really creative with stacking. Each display defied gravity and physics and I never, ever got the hang of building them. Every elaborate pyramid was topped with a display that tied in a piece of art, a flower arrangement or a lamp, and the product that was stacked precariously beneath it. No matter how I built the displays I was always told it was wrong. I looked perfectly fine to me and to this day I have no idea what I was missing. I was never told what exactly was wrong only "Do it again!" and I spent every day doing displays over and over and over.

Old women would come in and want decorating advice about lamps and art and curtains and sconces and I had no earthly idea about any of it. If I worked too long without taking a break I was yelled at. If I took a break I was yelled at for taking a break in the middle of a project. I was so miserable at that job every night I would go home and pray "God, get me out of that place."

Two weeks before Christmas, ONE DAY before my full pay and benefits as an assistant manager were to activate, I was fired. I was then out of work for a whole week. At the time it was the longest time I had been without a job in my life, since starting to work at age thirteen. I answered an ad in the paper advertising for a general manager for a a a store at the same mall. The name of the store was not given, only a 1-800 number. I called and talked to someone and then waited the longest four days of my life to get an interview. It took place in the food court, I wore my hair down and it was past my waist and copper penny red at the time. I think I wore the same tailored green dress I wore to my college graduation. I thought I was hired because of my degree but later I found out the company owner had no idea I'd even been to college.

The place was called Totally Nuts. It was a kiosk that sold almonds and pecans roasted in a heavenly smelling batter of cinnamon, sugar and vanilla, along with other coated nuts and candy. It was situated right inside the main mall entrance right between the Hot Topic and the FYE music store. My first co-workers were Marco and Diane, both high school students. They showed me the ropes.

=+=

Before I get to the day to day goings on at the mall, the equipment failures and the basic human stupidity I learned to deal with on a daily basis, I would like to tell you about the cast of characters I met when I worked there and how I became "mall mom" to some seventy odd kids who flocked to my stand once they realized I had a cd player stocked with good music and was willing to listen to them no matter what they had to say. Two players in this cast of dozens were Big Mike and Little Mike.

.Big Mike was my first "son"—mall son—he was the first kid I met at the mall. He passed by wearing a Son of Sam (the side project of AFI front man, Davey Havok) shirt and a blue mohawk. Remembering that mohawk I realize I probably knew him five years before I ever saw the real color of his hair. Having dyed my own hair from age 14 to 35, that was the first sign that we'd click.

Mike was the catalyst of my Punk Rock Midlife Crisis, the first person to tell me about AFI and Davey Havok, and part of the grease that set the wheels in motion for me to become straightedge.

He still calls me mom, I still have total strangers come up and say "You're Mike's mom aren't you? He told me about you." Though many followed him, I always call Mike my #1 son though I biologically have no kids and never will.

I was never technically old enough to be his mom. I joked that I had a wild affair with Glenn Danzig when I was 12 and Mike was the result. In Corpus Christi, this was completely believable.

MIke's real family mystified me. He had a German mother, an ex military father, a druggie brother and a sister. I knew his cousin Bill who was a great looking guy that played horror punk and fancied himself a big rock star as he made cds in his basement.

Now unless Mike had some murder, rape or mugging in his past I never knew about he was just a typical teenager, never arrested, never hard into drugs, never terribly rebellious beyond being and emo goth type. Yet Mike's parents kicked him out at age 16 and left him to fend for himself, while his other two siblings had their every whim catered to.

The first two years I knew him Mike lived his life on the streets, on people's couches, the back of pickup trucks. I never figured out why this was that he was shunned. But one day bemoaning his fate as a gutter punk he looked at me and said "Why couldn't YOU have been my mom?" and immediately, though I didn't think about it at the time, I blurted out "I'll be your mom! I'd be happy to be your mom. I'd love to have a son like you." and that's how it started.

Soon Mike was dragging all his friends over and introducing me as "mom" and I had this little army of mall kids under foot. There was Ben, Mary, Tommy, Marci, Karly, Julie, Robert, Tippy, TJ, and they all called me Mom too. Each year, a new group popped up as word spread and that's how I became mom to…last time I counted…70 kids.

Mike was always displaced, depressed, wearing black, threatening to kill himself and how he had nothing to live for. When he wasn't talking about suicide he was talking about Davey Havok. AFI was the band of choice I would come to find out for every kid who had ever been beaten, raped, neglected or abandoned. Davey Havok was nothing less than the incarnation of Jesus himself, promising salvation from all they had endured. I began to listen to AFI and love them because of Mike. AFI led to being curious about being edge, led to me watching the life of someone I admired and thinking "Wow, I want to be like that" and, against everything I knew and loved at the time, led me to make that commitment myself, it all started with Mike though he was never edge at all.

Everything turned around the day Big Mike met Little Mike. Little Mike was confined to a wheelchair and only had the use of one hand. He was two years younger than Big Mike but was into everything Big Mike was: goth music, AFI, hot punk chicks, and just doing the things boys that age did.

Big Mike and Little Mike became the Jay and Silent Bob of our mall. Little Mike earned the name "Speed Racer" by running down patrons in his motorized chair. They chased girls, especially Laura, one of my employees, they hassled people for change, bummed cigarettes, stole from Spencer's and Hot Topic. My husband ran the convenience store across the street from the mall back then and he knew them too.

Seeing this I guess, Little Mike's parents let Big Mike come live with them. Having dropped out of school before, Big Mike went back, enrolling with Little Mike. Soon they were never apart. Big Mike stayed in Little Mike's room, getting up in the middle of the night to carry him to the bathroom or get him water of he needed it. Little Mike got a best friend, Little Mike's parents got a free nursemaid, and Big Mike got food, a bed and the family he never had.

=+=

A bit after September 11th I took the bus to pay my insurance across the street from Little Mike's school. Big Mike wasn't there, I'm not sure why, but Little Mike was alone. We rode the bus back together and he told me how Big Mike was protesting how the 9/11 attacks were handled by the government and wanted to hang the family flag upside down as a sign of distress. His parents had told him if he did he wasn't getting any dinner so Big Mike relented and left the flag alone. We talked about more than that but for some reason that is the only thing I remember. I got off the bus, the sun was setting and I told him goodbye.

About a month later I ran into Big MIke on the bus home from work. Big Mike was coming home from school alone. I sat down beside him and I will never forget that he showed me the first picture I had ever seen of Davey Havok in his school notebook. He then turned to me and said:

"Mom, I think Little Mike is going to die. It's just typical. The one time I find a best friend and he's going to die."

Mike was the King of Exaggeration and I had long since learned to take what he said with a grain of salt.

"Now Mike what makes you say that?" I said, playing along.

"He's been sick all week. He hasn't been able to go to school. This morning I tried to wake him up to say goodbye and his eyes got all glassy. He could barely raise up his head. It took a long time before he said anything and he just said "Goodbye brother." and it sounded so final. I just...I really think he's going to die."

So, I turned to him and said in a condescending voice that I still hear in my own head: "Now honey, don't be silly. He probably just has the flu. He is NOT going to die."

As we were driven back to our respective homes though, Little Mike's kidneys were failing. Two days later he died.

Two days later, clueless, I got on the bus after work. The route was different back then, hitting the two high schools on Staples Street before the mall. I stepped in and as soon as I did, up the aisle ran Julie.

Julie.

I have not thought of her in years. She looked like Marisa Tomei, she had that huge smile. She was a bit out of her mind. She was so tiny but she was fierce. I remember walking with her to her job at the other mall (our malls are within six blocks of each other) and some guy stopping to offer us a ride. Probably because Julie was dressed like Stevie Nicks. So Julie says "You get up front, I'll get in the back behind the driver's seat. If he tries anything, I got a stiletto in my boot. I'll stab him in the neck!" The smile on her face told me she sort of hoped he would.

She dressed in these long, flowing black gowns. She was dating this boy who had a twin. She ended up having sex with his twin brother, getting pregnant and having an abortion because she wanted to get pregnant by the right brother. Which she did. After she had the baby I never saw her again. Never knew what happened to her.

That hot bright day though I stepped through the doors into the chill of the a/c on the bus and Julie floated up the aisle to me and took both my hands. That sticks with me. No one else ever reached for both of my hands at once like that. She pulled me all the way to the back of the bus where Jeremy, one of the twins, was waiting. We sat down and she squeezed my hands and said "Joey, Mike is dead."

The first thing I could think to say, the first thing I blurted out was "WHICH MIKE?!" I honestly expected it to be Big Mike because he always talked about killing himself. But no, it was little Mike, little Mike who would never walk, little Mike who never lived to see his 17th birthday.

Strangely it did not hit me until the bus stopped across from my apt. The minute Julie let go of my hands I began to sob. Everyone on the bus turned to stare at me but I didn't care. I cried all the way across the apartment complex, stopping and leaning on cars, got inside and collapsed on the floor. It was so unfair and so unexpected and I was mad at myself for what I had said to Big Mike which now seemed like the most unfeeling thing in the world. This was three years before I became edge and Axl Rosebush and I both drank quite a bit. I'm not sure how much alcohol we had, but we always had it on hand. I drank everything we had in the house and then staggered to the store across the street to buy more.

I remember having to get a shopping cart in order to stand upright and walk into the store. If anyone thought it was odd that I was using a whole shopping cart to buy two bottles of Boone's no one said anything. I have NO idea how I walked back home when I couldn't even stand. I do remember singing the song Hand Me Down My Walkin' Cane by Robert Earl Keen over and over at the top of my lungs that proclaimed "My sins they have overtaken me". I cannot hear that song now without just shuddering from the aura of grief that still infuses every single note.

=+=

I don't know why I picked that song but it made perfect sense drunk. When Axl Rosebush came home from work I ran to him, slobbering and crying and uttering the single most bizarre sentence I have ever uttered and never thought I would having never given birth:
"One of my kids is dead!!"
It would not be the last time I had to say those words either.

The rest are these blurred images, 30 second sound bites, a movie trailer of mourning: going to the viewing where they made Mike look like a 30 year old cholo, the quiet of the mall during the funeral that I couldn't attend because I had to work and no one could or would cover for me, the sight of the first kid to make it back from the funeral.

That was Ben. Ben would eventually lose my favor by marrying a girl and then cheating on her with a teenage hooker two weeks later and bragging about it to all his friends. But that was years after. I remember looking down the hall and seeing Ben, this tall, skinny, vision in black. Ben turned, saw me and made a run at me like he intended to spear me down to the ground. At the last second he burst into tears, grabbing me in a hug as he collided with me so hard we both nearly toppled over.

I never forgot that hug.

Big Mike was then back on the streets. His folks didn't care that he'd lost his best friend and Mike began to make good on all his promises to kill himself. He tried at least four times that I know of, probably more that I don't. Ben tried his best to take care of him but Mike would call Ben at work to say "I'm ODing right now, you might want to come home." Finally Ben had him committed. Ben and Mike came to see me before Mike got sent away and we all hugged and cried together. Ben and Mike came to see ME, they did not go to Mike's real mom.

Despite disowning Mike, his parents kept him on their insurance, and they had great insurance. Once the great beastly dragon of the MHMR world sank its claws into Mike and his beefy insurance policy, it wouldn't let go. He was in and out of the hospital for the next three years. Three years is a long time to be in that environment.

Every time I visited Mike, when it was time for me to go he would start to cry and beg me to stay a bit longer. I had never seen Mike cry before, even after Little Mike's death, but on all those pills, desperate for anyone to come and see him and not wanting me to go... after the first time I got used to it. The first time I walked out calmly, drove a block, pulled over and broke down myself because the vibrant, viciously funny, intelligent boy I knew had been reduced to a sweating, slobbering, slurring, scared and sobbing mess.

During this time I actually met Mike's real mom. I was expecting this two headed white trash hybrid of Britney Spears and that woman that drowned all her kids a few years back. But no, she was ten years older than me, well groomed, polite, heavy German accent and was head of the housewares department of Macy's. Why she decided she didn't give a rat's ass about her oldest son is beyond me. I never got it.

Even after he was released from the mental hospital Mike was not allowed home. He moved in with a girl for a while, she dumped him and he ended up in a homeless shelter for three years then moved on to a cheap motel where he, last I checked, worked maintenance in exchange for a room and barely enough money to keep from starving to death.

He exited the mental health system on 8 different pills a day, hearing voices in his head that he NEVER heard before being locked away and 180 pounds fatter than he was when he went in. Everyone commented on the weight gain. If you saw Mike on the street after he was released and knew him before, you would not have recognized him at all. He was enormous for no apparent reason. This was disturbing to me and I urged him to get his thyroid checked. It SHOULD have been disturbing to his parents but they didn't care. It took another three years before he began to faintly resemble the boy I knew in the Son of Sam shirt and blue mohawk. He never really came back to himself.

=+=

A while back I was reading an old copy of Rolling Stone on my lunch break. There was an article about how Eli Lilly began to work on a drug in the late 90's to calm schizophrenics. It was hailed as a miracle drug and when the patent on Prozac ran out, the MHMR industry needed another cash cow. The drug soon began to be pushed on anyone with any mental health issue, before realizing, years later, it was basically the same thing as Thorazine, a drug that turned it's patients into drooling, shuffling zombies.

The immediate side effect of this drug that they decided all their patients could live with? Extreme weight gain.

I now know what happened to Mike. His parents HAD to have noticed this, at some point and either they didn't ask the doctor about it or they were told that their son was being given experimental unproven drugs and they didn't give a shit.

I agree that it takes a village to raise a child, but sometimes it only takes one person, one person who truly gives a damn, and that person was me, someone Mike happened to meet from spending 9 hours a day in a mall and having no other place to go. The whole thing is fucking depressing.

=+=

Mike brought Ben, Ben brought Mary, Marci, and Karly. Then came Gabriel and Julie, and from then on it gets blurry because so many kids came and went. There were the Paladio sisters, one pretended to be misunderstood and cast out of a home with a drug addict mom when in actuality she just wanted the excuse to sleep with whomever she could to get what she wanted. The other pretended to be retarded. They both pretended to be poor and from a horrible home environment but I had no idea this was an act for many years and spent quite a bit of time and money trying to "save" them. There was Sarah and Daisey and a third Mike, two TJ's, Tippy, Kimmie and Emo Dave, then Dave's second girlfriend who's name I can't recall but who always had this deer in the headlights look and had a tattoo of the Thursday logo dove so low on her abdomen it was flying straight into her labia. There was Ameer and Kevin, the gutter punks, and Hope, the most intelligent of the bunch who spent her life being told she was nothing until she finally believed it and just gave up. There was also a boy named Robert who ended up getting the words MALL KIDZ tattooed across his back to commemorate the year we spent hanging out together. There was a Bill, two Crystals, two Amandas, Orlando, Jeremy.

These were just a few of the kids who popped up and began calling me mom. On top of this I became friends with a few of the kids who ran Hot Topic, with Jon and Mr. Chan of Chan's Imports next door to Hot Topic and of Greg, the manager of FYE. Lance, from the theater started a year or so after I did at the Walden Books just around the corner and chatting with him was always a treat because we both held very sarcastic views on life and considered ourselves far to intellectual to be working at a mall and yet there we were.

CHAPTER 13

Not all of my visitors at the stand were wanted.

There was Fred the creepy retarded janitor that tries to wink at me everyday and instead looks like he's having some kind of brain aneurysm, Then there were the kids screaming because either they want to go on the carousel, they're ON the carousel, or they're being dragged out the door while wanting to get on the carousel again! I always said why would I ever want to have kids when I had to deal with them eight hours a day anyway? The endless flow of kids on soccer/football/baseball teams that are allowed to beg for spare change to go to away games on was another annoyance. Although to be fair, NOW with the gas prices, they really do need the money. I swear before they probably just did it for fast food money.

Kids weren't the only agitation, adults were pretty nerve wracking as well.

The mall walkers watched my weight the way other people watch the stock market. There was the lady who manages Verizon next door whose laugh sounded like a cross between a hen being massacred and the wicked witch of the west.

Then I had my stalkers: The Tejano stalker and his anal sex jokes, He looked exactly like a walrus, had this huge grey mustache and glasses and was very hairy and just the single most unattractive man you can imagine. He actually laid out for me word for word what what he would do for me in bed. Ew."

The topper for most persistent was the Star Trek guy who was my age and still lived with his mom, who listened to Klingon Death Metal, read Shakespeare translated to Klingon and hit on me relentlessly for three years even though I told him I was married. One time while my husband and I were separated I finally broke down and asked if he could help me move my tv to my new apartment. His response was

"I'll have to ask my mom." so I said "forget it" and later used myspace to tell him to bugger off and never see me again.

=+=

Not all my stalkers wanted to have sex with me, some just wanted to bug me. Chief among these was the old man stalker with the handicapped daughter. This guy meant well I'm sure, he had an adult daughter who looked like she was thirteen, was profoundly retarded and was deaf and could not speak to communicate, only moaned and grunted. He took her every day to ride the carousel and every single day he would come up and talk to me about…nothing. He talked to hear himself talk. I'm sure he must have been lonely but seeing this man every single day for ten years was a bit much . During that time he never once having anything of any interest to say, it was just glorified babysitting for me.

Speaking of old men there were men who demanded samples every day and never once bought anything, For ten years. There was annoying manager of Eye Masters who would demand we break his big bills for him so he would not have to go to the bank,

Then there were the "lotion assholes" who have the territory staked out on the only route to the bathroom. They would grab your hand, give you lotion whether you wanted it or not and then launch into a hard sell on a $30 manicure kit. The only thing I hate worse that someone forcing me to buy something I don't need is someone I don't know grabbing me! The only thing I hate worse than someone grabbing me is someone grabbing me as I am running to the restroom because I have had to pee for three hours, I just now got a break in customers and I am leaving the stand guarded by some anonymous mall kid while I make a run for it. Sheesh.

The old men were the worst. One guy in particular I called "Moaning Myrtle" because I SWEAR to you, he whined every day and sounded exactly like that ghost in Harry Potter. He never actually STOPPED walking long enough to talk to you so he made power walk laps AROUND THE STAND as he talked, all the while MOANING about whatever. And he thought my name is Josey and god knows I was not going to correct him!

A typical conversation goes like this:

"OoOoOoOoooOoooOooooOOOoooh…Josey…I just got here to the mall and I'm only getting started, I've got two walk exactly 47 more minutes to get my hour in." or "OoOoOoOoooOoooOooooOOOoooh… Josey…what are you reading today? Are you getting any smarter? OoOoOoOoooOoooOooooOOOoooh…I'm going to want a book report from you when you're done."

CHAPTER 14

Three years in, I was already plotting my great escape. When times were slow there really wasn't much else to do. This could be a blessing and a curse. If a friend came by, you had the time to have the greatest conversations known to man. However if an idiot came by that you were not interested in and he was obviously just there to bug you and hit on you and not buy a thing, minutes could feel like hours and I would even welcome a visit from Fred the janitor just to save me from the idiot who was monopolizing my time. The funniest time waster I can remember was trying to figure out the most unlikely occurrence that could ever happen at the nut stand. We decided it was this: What if a Cajun man came in to try the Cajun mix, but upon trying it he realized it was nothing like real Cajun nuts were supposed to taste like. He starts complaining only he's speaking Cajun and we can't understand what he was saying. So he gets madder and the Cajun temper gets the best of him and he ends up destroying the entire stand because of the Cajun Mix. The funny thing was that about two years after that, when Hurricane Katrina happened (which wasn't funny at all), we had an influx of real Cajuns come by and not one of them complained about the Cajun Mix. I actually had a very surreal run in with a bunch of crazy Cajuns at another job, but I will get to that much later on.

Hilarity ensued because we made it. We made our own fun, much like children, which in many ways I had regressed into, being surrounded by so many kids, eight hours a day for ten years. Most of this hilarity was because of a girl named Amanda, whom I always called Dionysus because of her screen name. When she came along good times were guaranteed. She was a short term Joe Cole to my Rollins. My friend PJ is the real Joe Cole, my best friend for twenty five years. However PJ also lived up in Yankeeland, in Philadelphia, a million miles away from Texas. Di was my proximity Joe, and we never had more fun than we did at the mall. Whether it was nicknaming people, like the anorexic, over sexed girl who worked at Hot Topic that talked about her boobs all the time on myspace. The funny thing was, she didn't have boobs.

Gwyneth Paltrow with her bee stings had a bigger rack than this chick. This chick was aptly named "Skeletor". There was also Commie Chris who we imagined carried a Communist Party Discount Card. We would stand around at work telling each other, and passersby: "Da, comrade, we are having a GREAT day here in Mother Russia! Thank you for calling the Communist Discount Card Party Line. Please remember to use your Commie Discount card for an extra 25 percent wherever you shop. Look for the hammer & sickle on the door as a sign on the door of all the fine merchants who welcome the card."

No one else thought this was funny, they merely thought we were mentally disturbed.

I saw every manner of scene kid that ever existed. If you go to www.yourscenesucks.com—a site dedicated to drawing and defining every mall rat and scene kids imaginable—I waited on all those kids in person. One day Di and I see this kid. He was dressed in a tshirt of some hardcore band, wasn't wearing socks, and for some reason he has his pants rolled on one leg. We watched him and made note of his curious fashion sense. The longer he stayed in the mall, the more creative we became. We would smile at him, wait until he started to turn his back...3...2...1: bam! We'd start laughing again. **The 101 rules of Hardcore** had just come out online. If you have never seen the 101 Rules of Hardcore, google it. It is a handy guide to any poser who wants to fit in. Number five on the list stated: *5) Ankles are tough so bring your socks down into your shoes so we can see them.* Number 19 reiterates: *"More ankles, people!"* We are positive this kid has read, and is living by this list. After a while we notice that exposed leg is really shiny and appears to be shaved. Seeing this, we are now falling over each other, laughing. People are starting to stare at US because we are laughing at HIM so hard. This goes on for almost an hour. Finally he comes a little closer and we realize that his leg is not shiny because it is shaved...it's a prosthetic limb! As much as we were bagging on him, the kid was actually, legitimately hardcore. You can't get much more hardcore than a fake leg. Poor kid, we never saw him again but to this day, twelve years later, it makes me laugh.

Most of the time I read books, which was how I came to know Zeki and Hayat. Both are retired professors and both fled their upper echelon, literary, government approved lives when Sadaam Hussein seized power. Hayat was an English professor and Zeki had a doctorate in Mass Communications. Hayat would drop by to critique what book I was reading and tell me I need to read less "Popular trash" and more of the classics that would make me think. We ended up becoming very close and when they found out I was an orphaned half Arab they pretty much adopted me.

When I wasn't reading I was writing poetry or fan fictions or just imagining things.

=+=

ANY FOOL COULD DO THIS JOB!

Once I sat down and tried to figure out what the exact qualifications were to do my job. This is what I came up with.

To do my job you would have to be someone with experience in day care, who does not need mind the sound of screaming children for seven to eight hours a day. Between the kids begging for donations for softball, baseball and pee wee football at the community booth next door every day of every summer, unsupervised children grabbing bags and running with them, coming up as many as six or seven times for samples (and I have been cussed out on more than one occasion by parents for cutting their children off at FIVE samples) and the sound of kids screaming from the carousel they will be dealing with just as many children as adults.

Someone who is dependable. In the nearly ten years I worked there, the area where I was living flooded three times leaving my car under water to the door handles, each time I was without a car to drive. I was without a car twice due to wrecks and without a place to live once.

During all these times I was never once late for work, I showed up and the deposits got to the bank on time. Dependability is a must.

Someone who is bilingual as at least 80 percent of our customers have no comprehension of the English language.

Someone with the infinite patience to answer the exact same questions fifty times a day, every day, sometimes five to ten times for the same people for the above reason.

Someone able to display said infinite patience and politeness during the following scenarios(these did not happen occasionally, they happened every single day, multiple times most days):

Customer: "What's that great smell?"
Me: "It's the bavarian pecans, they have cinnamon sugar and vanilla on them."
C: "Can I have the vanilla ones?"
M: "It's cinnamon sugar and vanilla, it's all together."
C: "what do the prailines have on them?"
M: "Just sugar"
C: "So it's the same thing."
M: "No, the prailines have sugar the bavarian have cinnamon sugar and vanilla. I have the bavarians in almonds, pecans, cashews and peanuts."
C: What's the difference between a pecan and an almond?

Or

Customer: I want some nuts.
Me; What kind?
Customer: The sweet kind.
Me: All we sell are sweet kinds except for the Cajun mix.
Customer: the sweet nuts.

Me: what kind of nuts, we have almonds, pecans, cashews and peanuts.

Customer: I don't know. The sweet ones you always have. I don't remember what kind I just know they were sweet.

[like going to a restaurant and saying "I do not know what I usually purchase here. I just know its MEAT!]

-Or-

C: (puts hand in sample cup and begins picking): Can I have a sample?

M: Uh, yeah…go ahead (your hand is already in it!)

C: What is this?

M: That is the Bavarian Pecan (points to CLEAR LARGE sign that says BAVARIAN PECANS $3.25 PER BAG OR TWO FOUR $6).

C: (Looks at sign, looks at basket of pecans.)

So its an almond?

M: No, its a pecan.

C: How much is it?

While this exchange is taking place a second customer has been watching and hears everything.

C 2: (pointing from brown, shiny pecan in sample cup to the basket of orange and red colored cajun mix next to it) *So are these uns these uns here?*

C: I want the Banana Pecans.

M: The Bavarian ones?

C: No, it says here Banana.

M: That says Bavarian.

Q: What's that great smell?

A: The Bavarian pecans

C: You put BLUEBERRIES ON THEM?

A: No, it's Bavarian. It's cinnamon, sugar and vanilla.

Q: But what's on it?

A: Cinnamon, sugar and vanilla

Q: So what's a Bavarian?

Q:"What's the difference between a salted almond and a chocolate almond?"

A: Uh…a chocolate almond has CHOCOLATE on it!

Or looking at a prailine pecan which CLEARLY is covered in WHITE POWDERED SUGAR and asking

Q:"Are these chocolate!?"

A: They're white and crusty!! Does that look like chocolate to you?!

Then there was my favorite: the multi chambered sample tray: We'd have bavarian almonds (brown and football shaped), praline pecans (white, powdery, flat circles), chocolate almonds, and cajun mix (orange and yellow colored) for people to try.

People would look at the tray and say

"Is this all the same thing?"

DOES IT REALLY LOOK THE SAME?! ARE YOU COLOR BLIND?!

Q: (Holding up a bag clearly marked ALMONDS)

"Are deez de only kind a' peanuts ju got?"

A: No, those aren't peanuts, those are almonds. We have 15 different kinds.

Q: "Yeah but are deez de only kind a' peanuts ju got?"

Q: What are these?

A: Chocolate cashews

Q: But what's in 'em? Peanuts or sumthin?

A: Uh, no. They're called chocolate cashews because they have CASHEWS inside them.

Q: What's a cashew?

"Can I have some nuts?"

What kind?

"I dunno. Nuts."

This is like going to a restaurant and asking for a MEAT SANDWICH!

What KIND of meat: meatloaf, bologna, ham, turkey, deer meat, lamb, bacon, pork, steak??

This probably seems humorous to you, but dealing with it on a daily basis for more than eight years was not.

Getting back to my job, if I was to be replaced, you would need to hire someone who did not mind monotony and can repeat the phrase *"I'm sorry, we're out of that.",* and put up with customer complaints while keeping a smile on their face as we were almost never stocked completely on everything it took to run the stand. They should also be prepared for the roaster to break every 90 days.

Someone who is male would be ideal, as I was stalked and sexually harassed by all manner of old men and a few young ones as well. And since I could only call security if someone was in the act of stealing from me, I endured nearly ten years of every type of dirty joke, sexual innuendo, play on the word "nuts" and comments on my hair, body, clothes and make up. None of these things would happen to a man. Since I was in sales and dealt with the public I had to smile and laugh it off when I wanted nothing more than to kick 99% of these men in THEIR nuts and not the ones they bought from us!

Speaking of clothing…Someone with a vast array of filthy work clothes would be a good candidate because most of their day will be spent on the floor on their hands and knees in any number of awkward positions pulling boxes from the cabinets. A strong back and good knees will be helpful too.

They need to be muscular to haul the roaster across town when it breaks like clockwork every 90 days. Once our owner switched from Fed Ex to Central Freight because it was cheaper, the delivery person no longer put our stock inside the stand. It was dumped, three boxes high and five boxes deep on a palette in the middle of the mall and I had to take all 15-30 boxes, weighing 25-50 lbs a piece and put them in the stand and haul the palette to the dumpster myself. It was the same with Sysco, whom the boss went with over Ben E. Keith to save money. They dump 600 pounds of sugar in 50 pound bags outside the stand and I had to unload and stack them myself. I considered myself to be in good shape then, but it was ridiculous. Since I never knew when stock would show up (or if it would show up at all), it was impossible to schedule anyone to help me.

Someone with personnel skills and a touch of ESP would help when hiring people. Basically, in my experience, there are two types of people: Those who are about as dumb as rocks but who are reliable and honest, or those who are intelligent and highly motivated…to steal from you. You can either have someone who shows up every day on time and does absolutely nothing or have someone who is great with customers but is always late or calling in or who's money is always off

CHAPTER 15

Many things happened while I worked that job. I free-lanced as a writer for a while, driving 5 hours to and from McAllen to sit in on production meetings of a tiny little independent paper that eventually went under. I turned thirty and being stuck between F.Y.E and Hot Topic and surrounded by kids half my age plummeted me head first into what I can only describe as my "punk rock midlife crisis". I'll get much further into this later. During this time I turned straightedge, went from a size 13 to a size 4, read the works of Marx and Lenin for the first time, and tried out being a vegetarian, I did a tandem sky dive, rediscovered punk music and discovered hardcore for the first time and finally got to have the teenage years I never had the first time around.

The mall life could be taxing but the pay was amazing. For the first time in my life I could afford manicures, massages and a gym membership. In fact, I got hooked on the gym and that's what part of what kept me a size four for so long. During that time my husband worked the opposite shifts as me and needed the car to deliver pizzas. This was back when gas was ninety nine cents a gallon, it was truly the boom times. During those times this is what a typical day was for me.

I'd wake up at 5 am, mix the perfect sugar to milk to coffee ratio, get online for an hour as back then I was just beginning to pick up friends in the realms of A.F.I, My Chemical Romance, and WWE fan fiction. Leave for the gym at seven with a great mix of songs on the Ipod shuffle which is now completely obsolete, with generic mp3 players holding twice as much as the model my husband paid two hundred dollars to buy for me one Christmas, Run two miles (I never ran in my life before losing that weight), go to the bank, do my deposit, and go home. At home I shower, wash my hair, brush my teeth, shave and change, eat, and pack a lunch. Most days I could do this in forty five minutes. Then there was the mad dash to the bus stop to catch the bus for work. And it was certainly a good day when I can do my makeup without poking myself in the eye with the mascara wand. I do this even when I am looking in the mirror as I seem to have NO depth perception.

However, no matter how good the morning starts out, the instant I walked through the doors of the mall, any good day I was having went directly to hell.

It was like I am living the movie **Groundhog Day** where I went through the same day every day FOR NINE YEARS.

I knew the same people will smile at me, the same people will scowl at me, the same old men would try to grope me on their morning mall walk. The same people would take samples without ever buying a bag, the same people would bitch if there were no samples out for them to take without ever buying a bag.

The same mall walker would show up between noon and one and either complain that my register tape is too long or too short. If I was reading a book he would sarcastically ask for a book report, demand a sample and then tell me in minutes and seconds how long he has to go before he completes the hour he walks EVERY DAMN DAY. No matter how rude I was, no matter how short with him I tried, even when I outright ignored him he still never got the hint that he was the single most annoying fuck I had ever had the displeasure of meeting.

The same black guys would come in singing or rapping at THE TOP OF THEIR LUNGS, all the way through the mall for the duration of their visit, as if they really and truly expected Clive Davis or Dr. Dre to have record scouts hanging out at the Padre Staples Mall in Corpus Christi Texas just waiting to snap up talent like it is the hip hop capital of the world.

The manager of Spencer's would give me the same dirty look he had given me every morning for five years when he went to open. I've never met the guy in my life, never spoke to him, but five years ago one of his employees was using the store to deal drugs out of. Not only this but he had told me a friend of mine who had been drugged and raped deserved it and "a girl passed out on a bed isn't rape, that's a good Friday night".

So I had put up an online post via myspace offering to pay anyone who'd fuck up his shit and take his drug money. I didn't want the money but I sure as hell didn't want him enjoying it either. No one ever took me up on it but enough people saw it. From that time until the day I quit, his boss would shoot me daggers every single time he walked past.

And the few things it did change never changed for the better.

When I started Hot Topic played The Ramones, The Misfits and AFI. By the end of my tenure they played bands put together, manufactured, promoted and sent on tour solely to be played in Hot Topic stores. It is almost as if The Monkees and the GAP had an unholy alliance.

CHAPTER 16

If you could possibly make a mash up of "**For the Workforce, Drowning**" by Thursday and "**Every Day is Exactly The Same**" by NiN it would be the story of the last 8 years working at the mall.

When I started as the general manager there, the average monthly gross was six thousand a month. When I left, it was eighteen thousand a month but the owner still thought it wasn't enough. Nothing was ever enough for him. One Christmas ago, during our busiest time, my husband was suicidal. One night I stayed up all night with him to try and keep him from killing himself. At 8 am he tried anyway and I had to take him to the ER and leave him because I had to go in to work. We had an order for 150 gift tins to be picked up that day and I wanted to see it done personally so no one would botch the sale or take off with the money. I worked my entire shift though I was crying through half of it. That month we made nearly $38,000 but I did not hear one word of thanks.

Years before that, I got a paycheck that was unusually large. I called the office before cashing it and asked "Has there been a mistake made? There was way too much on my check this time." I was told "No, there was no mistake, the extra $300 is your monthly bonus." I said "But we didn't meet our sales goal. Are you sure this is right?" "Yes," I was told, "go ahead and cash it.", so I did. I could have kept the bonus all for myself but I split it equally with Diane and Laura who worked for me at the time. The next time I spoke to the owner I was stupid enough to open my big mouth and said "Thank you so much for the bonus even though we didn't quite make our sales goal." He yelled at me and demanded that I give the money back immediately. I couldn't do this because 2/3 of it had already been given away. I CALLED, I ASKED, and a representative told me it was okay to cash that check. That made the mistake theirs.

Yet the next time I got paid $300 came out of MY check even though I only took $100 for myself. Nothing was taken out of Diane's or Laura's. So I had to survive two weeks on a FRACTION of what I normally got on my paycheck. I did not get the money I earned all because of a mistake the company made. My only mistake was being stupid enough to say thank you and having the integrity to call attention to it to begin with. Any other person would have taken the money, kept it all to themselves and the boss would have been none the wiser.

CHAPTER 17

Not all my memories about the mall were of being exhausted, overworked and stalked. I became a "mom" to over seventy kids. Working in a place between an FYE and a Hot Topic, blasting AFI cds, kids sort of converged on my place of business. They influenced me, I influenced them, I hope both for the better. I got to play at being a mom, I got to know what it feel like to be needed and hopefully they got to know what it was like to have someone who actually listened and cared.

MY MALL KIDS
Andy-Eric-Tippy-Toria-Amanda1-Hope-Sarah-Mary-Marcie-Mike-Nikki-
Karly-Gabe-TJ-George-Gilbert-Ben-Lil Mike (deceased)-"Fluffy" Chris-
Emilie-Kim-Chris (David and Bianca's friend)-Dave with Gauges-Ameer-Skinny Mike-Kevin-Gay Mike-Zeke—Marc-Eli-Katie-Jeremy-Maren-Charles-Bill-Crystal1—Rich-Crystal2-
The Kid-Roger-Kris-Daisy-Matt-Tommy(deceased)-Sloth-Sergio-JJY-Ashley-
Emo Dave-Cheyenne & Tommy-Julie-Robert-Dave from Sounds of the Underground-
Larissa-Jason from the Danzig show-Mikey's cousin Brandon-Billy Bob-Amanda2-Viv-Glenn-Ronnie-Charles-Mike Im-Debra-blond Jason-Perryman-Stevo-Dylan-Chase-Chazz-James' friend Robert-Jakob-Nicole-Tanya-Rubenn-Surfer TJ-InsaneCrystal-Jackie-Randy-Orlando-Annie-Erica-Corey-Nate-Izzzy-Max-Isaiah—Danny-Roy-Erika-Brent-Gay Mark-sXe Chris2

Of all 90 or so:

2 have been to Iraq and come home
2 are dead

4 have been in jail/prison (probably more than that)
2 have spent more time IN a mental institution than out
1 has "Mall Kidz" tattooed across his back
1 is a stripper
2 finished college and got degrees
1 is a successful tattoo artist
I've lost count of who all has kids.
Mary and Karly still called me Mom until I lost touch with them, Crystal and Hope called me Mama Joey and before I quit, Mike would call every week to say "*Hey Mama, how's it going?*", and say goodbye by saying "*I love you Mom*". For seven years he introduced me to everyone as "My foster mom".

When Crystal would come by she would bring her daughter "Sunshine Peach" and says "Say hello to Mama Joey" and when the little girl would wave it would be the happiest feeling in the world. I am a Mall Grandma to 4 kids that I know of.

I befriended, mentored and tried to help another dozen or so kids I met online, girls like The girl who called herself Mikey Way, who called herself Mikey, a girl who called herself The generic scene girl from Austin (both whose real names I never knew), a girl whom I nicknamed The girl who loved Jade Puget because she loved Jade Puget, a delusional girl named Rachel who called herself Shin Solo. They were the first. There was also Naz, a girl who wanted to be a boy, Pasha, whom I never really knew other than as a livejournal buddy, and dozens more I met through AFI and My Chemical Romance fan communities. I loved them all, I miss them all. Two, Aidan and Renee, who called themselves Kitty and Fishy online, respectively, are still family to me and occupy a piece of my heart that will house them alone until the day I die.

=+=

The kids planted the seeds within me: the seeds of wanting to teach, of wanting to save the world, of wanting to leave something more behind than just my myspace page. When it came down to it, the only thing I really and truly loved about the job at the mall was hanging out with the kids, Because of them I finally got to have a childhood. We chased each other through the mall chunking confetti at each other each time one of the members of AFI had a birthday. They let me tag along with them to clubs and concerts, they gave me my own entourage of minions and I loved them. For the first time in my entire life I felt included and accepted and not some freakish cast off that no one understood.

THE BANDS

During my time at the mall I discovered three life changing bands: AFI, Rise Against and Throwdown. At first AFI was my favorite. Because of AFI I turned straightedge, because of AFI i wanted to change the world. I listened to every sob story of every kid I knew and did everything I could to help them. It never occurred to me that they could be lying to me, all I knew was that they needed my help. Because of writing AFI fan fiction I met four girls whom, as I mentioned before, became like my real daughters, Renee, The generic scene girl from Austin, Kitty and The girl who loved Jade Puget. Ten years later, Renee and Aidan are the only ones, not just out of those three but of literally hundreds of AFI fans I knew online that I still communicate with and that still calls me mom.

Three bands shaped that time in my life more than any other bands since I was impressionable and in high school. Well I regressed back to high school age and became just as impressionable during the days of my midlife crisis. I was heavily influenced by friends, song lyrics and got my heart broke almost every day but was healed by the music that was so close to my heart. '

I will now tell the story of the girl who loved Jade Puget and the generic scene girl from Austin (again, I could not use their real names without permission and they are long since gone from my life) and my journey to being straightedge, but I can't do that without talking about the bands that led me, guided me, influenced me, comforted me and sang me to sleep. First there was AFI.

CHAPTER 18

I started listening to AFI when Sing The Sorrow came out, after having been told about them several times from a guy named Chris I was terribly enamored of who worked next door at Hot Topic. He, and pretty much everyone else under the age of twenty, seemed to live in AFI t shirts and and one day I had to walk up and ask "Um, what does AFI stand for?" He told me and slowly I began to work my way back through the cds, but once I got **Black Sails**, and heard Last Kiss, something just snapped.

Everything on Black Sails was excellent (and thank god singer Davey Havok put lyrics in the sleeve because he screams so fast you can't catch it a lot of the time), but that song, Last Kiss, hit me so hard and brought back so many memories I wasn't ready to deal with, it just freaked me out. I don't remember any song every coming out and dealing with self-mutilation the way that song did. To say I could relate was an understatement.

My mom died when I was twelve and my dad quickly remarried and my life became an unending nightmare from then on. It was abusive, it was horrendous, it was unending. Do you know what it's like to be scared 24 hours a day every single day of your life for seven or eight years? Do you know what it's like to have the only communication with your "parents" come in the form of being called every name you can imagine and being threatened with being locked in a mental institution because they don't like the type of music you listen to? And back in those days I listened to those famous Satanists and rebel-rousers... **Dokken**.

=+=

Do you know what it's like to only get 2-3 hours of sleep at night (and have to go in prepared for high school the next day) because your "parents" are in the other room half drunk and trying to cave each other's skulls in? I know it all.

Every single day I dreamed about killing myself until that was all I thought about. I could either kill myself or run away, but if I stayed I was convinced I would just snap and they would find me one day, under my bed, foaming at the mouth and so lost in my own head I'd never find my way out. And this sounded like a pretty nice way to go.

Though I prayed and went to church and read the Bible, I honestly expected for my roof to open up one day and the golden hand of God to come down and pluck me from my suffering. I just didn't realize it doesn't work that way and soon began to lose my faith. Davey Havok sang on Sing The Sorrow of wasting away, both physically and in faith while waiting for a reprieve from abuse that never came in the song The Great Disappointment. I knew he knew how I felt. Some references were not that vague and left nothing of the subject matter to be doubted. In the song Now The World, Jade Puget sings in the backing vocals of thriving on self-mutilation. It was all there, put forth for public consumption; someone knew the darkest secrets of my soul.

Before AFI was ever thought of however, I was suffering in silence in West Texas. When it all got too hard to deal with I would put in a certain tape and listen to a certain song over and over. The tape was by a musician out of Austin who was about the same age as me. The song was called "Don't Look Back" and it was about escaping. And once I learned that I'd never physically escape what was happening to me, the best I could do was leave in my mind and that song helped to do just that. What made me decide to try sneaking a kitchen knife into my room and slicing up my ankles for the first time is another story for another time, but that was the start of something.

This was 1989 before anyone talked about self-mutilation, hell now there are movies of the week on it. I was convinced my parents were right and I truly needed to be locked up, but god it felt good! Further in the song The Great Disappointment Davey talks about how he would make a wish and bleed. He didn't have to say he was cutting himself to draw this blood, but I felt I knew first hand he was.

There was something so righteous and so powerful about the knowledge that I could spill my own blood. It was the only thing in my life I had control of and it ruled. It was either **that** or hanging myself in my closet, and I really had no guts. So I made cuts deep enough to bleed with a kitchen knife and as soon as they healed I'd reopen them with a razor blade. I didn't do drugs, I didn't drink, I was a virgin until I was 26. I didn't know what the hell Straight Edge was until I was in my late 20's. That didn't exist in my hometown. I read about it in magazines in college and even then, I thought it was a musical style, and not a way of life.

I didn't kill myself. I didn't drink myself to death. I didn't fuck everything that moved. I didn't end up in an institution. I did cut myself an awful lot and listened to Don't Look Back by Charlie Sexton while doing it. Because of that, I lived.

=+=

My dad died when I was 20 and my step mom moved away and suddenly the abuse was gone and I was left alone to deal with the scars and the reality that I'd survived and the guilt that maybe all the bad thoughts I'd ever thought of my dad caused the cancer that killed him. My dad died a week before Christmas in 1991 and as a Christmas present for 1992 my big sister bought me a ticket to see that musician for the first time. He was fronting a band called The ARC Angels and they were playing the Agora Ballroom in Dallas TX.

Whenever I hear This Celluloid Dream I go right back to that night. I drove for five hours to see that show and wading through the crowd into the front row and looking into his eyes for the first time was nothing short of a religious experience for me. The entire night was dreamlike and the only thought I can remember thinking was "This is what it's like to feel happy, like I belong."(with all erased).

I hadn't felt happiness in so long, it had been so long since I had felt anything other than pain and fear, it was almost too overwhelming for words. As I stepped out the door when the show was over, I looked up to the sky to say a prayer of thanks, the first time I could remember being truly thankful in so long. As I looked up, it began to snow and I stood there with it swirling all around me, not feeling a thing, other than joy to be still alive. On a freezing note, that night I resonated and all the color became grey then turned Technicolor again and I began to live.

I realized I was alive, had all my mental faculties intact and knew that a good reason for this was the music that had seen me through. I had to thank this guy somehow for keeping me from killing myself and helping me escape even if it was only in my mind for three and a half minutes at a time. I wanted something big, something to show for all I had gone through and all I had survived. And since I was hardly the groupie type and didn't look like Angelina Jolie, waiting for him backstage with a beckoning glance was totally out of the question.

I saved up a few hundred dollars while working three jobs to put myself through college. I took the money and sat still and in great pain for four hours while his likeness was tattooed on my shoulder. This earned me more hell from people in my small hometown than I would have gotten if I had murdered someone. Was I a lesbian? Was I in a gang? Who the hell was this guy and why was he on my shoulder blade? Did I not know that no man would ever marry a girl who had tattoos? And my all-time favorite stupid question "Did you get a marker and draw that on there yourself?" Yes Davey, from what I've seen, I hate humanity too.

Wanting more pictures to add more detail to the tat, I wrote into an Austin paper and my letter, along with a picture of the tattoo was published and I soon met a photographer willing to help me in any way he could. Feeling proud and quite full of myself, I bought as many backless shirts as I could find and took off for a gig in Austin where said musician was fronting yet another band.

I kept my hair cut short then and people kept stopping me to look at the design. Two very nice looking preppy guys even stopped me and asked if they could *shake my hand*. No one had EVER asked me that before. I was dancing it up in the front row and when the last song ended several people started screaming to get the musician's attention. When he looked down they grabbed me, turned me around and screamed "Look at her tattoo." which he did, and looked rightfully surprised. I floated out of that club that night, don't think my feet touched the ground once.

What new friend did that night bring? I was one of one thousand he was acquainted with that night. A photographer friend even took a picture of the tattoo, had it blown up and had the musician autograph it for me as a gift. The photographer asked him what he thought and he said it really freaked him out and kinda scared him that anyone would do that. I figured some day I'd have to tell him exactly why I did it, I didn't want him to think I was stalking him after all.

Ten years went by and a friend of mine who lives in Philadelphia was hanging out in a bar in New York: **PJ :** "So I'm out with Linda and we're at this bar in New York and there's this guy standing there a couple of feet away. I look over at him and he looks so damn familiar. I can't place where I'd seen 'im. I am wracking my brain. So I stare at him and he stares at me and this goes on for a while and then it hits me: THAT'S THE DUDE JOEY HAS ON HER BACK!!"

So she goes to talk to him and he does remember seeing the tattoo and still has the same thing to say, that it totally freaked him out. He wouldn't discuss it further other than to say "Hey, small world." Ten years later that's what he remembered. So while I should be happy that he remembered at all, something occurred to me: I would never be able to tell him why I got that tattoo, even in the terribly unlikely event that I would meet him and have the chance to talk.

If my getting a *tattoo* freaked him out, how on earth could I ever tell him what I was doing while I was listening to his music? Or that doing that was only the alternative to out and out ending my life?

So it hit me that while I will go through life counting him as one of my heroes and the best musician of our generation, he will go through life assuming I am some whacked out freak.

What does this have to do with **AFI**? When I bought my first cd I'll never forget opening it and reading inside not only where they recommended their fans get tattooed, but a special section THANKING the fans who already had AFI tattoos. *Thanking the fans?* Understanding that sometimes music touches you so deeply inside and changes your life to the point that you want the entire world to know it every time they look at you? What a concept!!

=+=

I currently have 29 tattoos and I would get every single one of them again, including the one of him.

My first straightedge tattoo, to commemorate my first six months edge was AFI related. It was an amalgam of the AFI icon wings from the inside of Sing The Sorrow, and an X to symbolize my commitment to being sXe for the rest of my life. The X has a halo over it a tribute to the logo of CM Punk's first tag team The Second City Saints.

Should I ever have the privilege of showing the men of AFI, I know I will be looked on with nothing less than respect and understanding. And if no one else on this earth gets why I did it, there are four people that will.

AFI's music means being comfortable in my own skin, dealing with my past and knowing it made me stronger and being so glad I never killed myself when I had the chance. It's being able to say I am "honored by your hatred". It means paying more attention to what I do to my body, what I put into it, trying to have respect for myself as well as the world around me. Doing all this even though I'm hated by my family, even though no one else understands except my husband and a slight handful of others

One Halloween I dressed up like Neil Gaiman's Death and Chris from Hot Topic mentioned above dressed like one of the Misfits. We were handing out candy at work and he asked about the tattoo on my shoulder. "It's just this musician from Austin," I mumbled, feeling very self-conscious under his gaze. "No one knows who he is." Chris looked at me and said "But if you know who he is, isn't that all that matters?" It was the simplest thing in the world, but boy did it make complete sense. He's an AFI fan, go figure.

I was on display and I was becoming and I became and became and became greater. I became straightedge, I learned to love myself. I learned to be my own hero. AFI's music was the cause of this. That is what AFI's music means to me.

CHAPTER 19

When I became straightedge, the first actual straightedge band I began to follow and the only one I stayed with was Throwdown, the epitome of the tough guy hardcore bands. I saw them five times in concert but the second time I saw them, at my favorite venue, The White Rabbit in San Antonio, is ingrained in my mind as the greatest night of my life.

BLOG ENTRY: THE NIGHT I SANG WITH DAVE PETERS
Well, as expected, two hours or so before we are supposed to leave, Axl Rosebush decides he does not want to go with me. He tells me to call up one of the mall kids and ask one of them to go.

The idea of driving myself…3 hours.by myself…to an unfamiliar venue…by myself…in a city I don't exactly know…by myself to wait in line…by myself…go inside…by myself…and walk in…by myself IS ABSOLUTELY HEART ATTACK INDUCING!!
But I have gone farther by myself—to Austin to see AFI—This wasn't NEAR as bad as that.
I go to the mall but of all the idiots usually hanging out there, not one will accompany me even with an extra ticket.

So fuck it, I left. An hour behind schedule, thanks to waiting around thinking Marc or Eric were going with me.
And what do I do when I get in the car? I catch my purse on my open bottle of Sobe and pull THE ENTIRE CONTENTS of the bottle into my lap!!
Not that I'm not EXCITED TO SEE DAVE PETERS…just not THAT excited!
But I have a 3 hour drive to dry my crotch.
Though I didn't have a single panic attack, I did have stomach churning nausea from nerves for the entire 2.75 hour drive that nearly made me turn back several times.

I kept telling myself "Gary said they went on around 9 or so. All I have to do is keep from puking for 3 more hours!"

Got to San Antonio, found the venue easy as anything! It was crazy how easy I found it.

Got in line.

Waited.

At 7:45 I was still waiting outside to get in. Something told me Throwdown was NOT going to go on at 8:45 or 9. Our plan had been: drive down, get there at 9, see Throwdown and leave. So this was my first indication it was a good thing Axl Rosebush did not go, he would have been PISSED already.

The venue was small but decent. I thought the bouncers and staff were nice and cordial but the pit begged to differ the entire night. I had will call tix and was thinking "Okay, I have one extra, I can hang it on my wall or get it signed.". Nope all they did was mark my name off a list.

I grabbed a Big Red on the way in and had I known it would be the only thing I'd have to drink the entire night because once you got to the front, getting to the back and up again was physically impossible, I would have gotten more. But hey.

So I'm looking around and the venue looks pretty cool. I find a spot next to the wall and at first the crowd doesn't look too bad....

Until the first band goes on and every single space in that club is filled with people.

The first band was **The Agony Scene**. Next to TD they were the best band of the night.

They were just great. I stood next to the wall on the side and the lip of the pit came all the way over to me during their set. Now that was fun!!

The next band to come on was **The Red Chord**.

Um...okay...about them...

Have you seen the Chappelle show episode with John Mayer?

You know the part where they're in the barber shop and Dave says "Latinos will listen to anything if it has an electric piano and people screaming nonsense over it." and he just starts screaming gibberish into a bullhorn?

THAT IS EXACTLY HOW THE RED CHORD SOUNDED!!!

I burst out laughing and everyone was like "Yeah!! Fuck Yeah!" and I'm thinking "You gotta be kidding me!"

It was like the teacher in Peanuts gargling mouth wash!!

But I will say the music was okay, they were funny as shit between songs and the bass player did an impromptu headbang Jam that just kicked ass. So they were okay in my book, NOT that I am going to ever pick up a cd of theirs.

But during their set I am standing to the side and I glance over and there is *this guy.*

He looked a bit like sXe Chris and you know me and that Elvis Costello archetype…*glance over…hmmm…dark hair…dark eyes…buzz cut…glasses…hoodie…vaguely Elvis Costello—ish…dingdingding!.*we have a winner!!!

I start to check him out.

From the neck up he looked like sXe Chris.

From the neck down he looked like BUDDAH!!!!!!!!!!!

It. Was. Disturbing!

Take the best looking guy you know and give him a Buddah belly!! Eeeek!

I decide that I don't wanna be that close to SweatyBuddahChrisGuy who appears to have the word "Heartburn" tattooed Jade Puget style across his gargantuan stomach. I start to move slowly away.

Okay two bands down. Now everyone has told me The Black Dahlia Murder is closing the show so if that's right then Throwdown has to be next.

I fight my way to the front row. The roadies are setting up and the band is coming out. The band is NOT Throwdown.

Okay, here comes the dilemma…should I stay or should I go now?

I've heard a lot about **The Black Dahlia Murder**, good and bad and I'm curious. So I stay.

The lead singer comes out.

Holy crap! It's *the guy—the amalgam of sXe Chris and Buddha I was checking out before.* I have to laugh.

It is at least 120 degrees inside that club. I am not even exaggerating. You are basically breathing humidity borne of the sweat of about 900 people in one enclosed area. Now don't get me wrong, they had tons of fans and there were pockets of air, but it was still FUCKING HOT.

So back I go. For a long while at random points of the night I was trying to get photos and basically just fucking around with Axl Rosebush's digital camera which he let me borrow. It's small, it's cheap, and you have to hold it ultrasteady or everything is a blur.

But there is this drunk asshole who is hitting on all the girls, single or not. He's been doing this all night and I have been watching. He is middle aged, he is white, he is dressed like a frat boy and hanging off of Death Metal listening to, Slipknot shirt wearing Mexicans like he is their best friend and head banging with them. He does NOT need to be at a show like this.

As I come back from the front of TBDM, he hones in on me and puts his arm around me and asks if I'm there alone. I give him a dirty look and dive back into the crowd.

Some people adore TBDM, some people say they suck live. They were okay with me. I would have had more of an opinion, but I was mesmerized by the singer's jiggling flab. Again, they were good with the audience so they were okay in my book but I still thought The Agony Scene was better.

Okay, they leave.

HOOORAY!

It's 11:20 pm, a time when on any other night I'd be in bed sound asleep. I can't even believe I'm here. When I saw this listed on myspace my heart just broke because I wanted to go with every fiber of my being and I was so sure it wouldn't happen. I never thought I'd actually be there.

Well, god bless the drunk—because of running away from him and into the crowd, I was in the perfect spot when TBDM finally left the stage and Buddha went back to blessing people or whatever it was he does. As soon as the crowd thinned I HURLED myself at that stage. I ended up FRONT and CENTER with only one guy who was exactly my size in front of me.

I slid a hand up under his arms and held on to the stage for dear life. With the other hand I reached for my digital camera to start taking pix of the stage set up.

Guess what?

I spent so much time and effort in vain to try and capture the paradox that WAS the Buddah/Chris guy from TBDM, I have completely used up my battery. I cannot even turn the camera on. I am about to be literally INCHES away from Throwdown and I cannot take one single photo.

DamnitDamnitSonofABitch!!!

The lights go down to the chants of the band's name from the crowd. The crowd surges, I'm pressed forward, I cannot move and I wouldn't have had it any other way. I've got a hold of the stage, my feet are planted, and I am ready. I don't know it then, but it is about 6 minutes away from one of the greatest moments of my life.

I'm already reeling because I am really there. To show you that I am not in my right mind...

It is STILL 120 degrees and I have now donned my Throwdown hoodie so I look exactly like my myspace photo. I have no clue who in the band I have been conversing with but I'm going to be prepared. Like I am going to be recognized anyway!!

I cannot tell you what Throwdown and their music mean to me.

My first year of edge was horrible. It was a test. I was miserable, scared and alone for most all of it. I had no real support, I felt utterly lost and abandoned and every single person I met that I thought was going to be my friend…wasn't. At least not most of them.

The only thing THE ONLY THING I HAD TO KEEP ME STRONG was this music. And it did and I am still here.

When it comes to the subject of being straightedge, the people I respect most: **Davey Havok, Chris and Dave Peters**. And that is it. Yes, there is McKaye, but that was not my experience, that was not my generation of being edge. I wasn't edge in the 80's or 90's. Dave wrote the lyrics that kept me alive. Other than those I've mentioned, NO ONE is on that level.

Dave Peters…
The lights went down and he was pacing like a caged animal right in front of me, shirtless, sweating and ready to pounce.

Suddenly I am in the middle of a sweating, screaming, stage diving mass of humanity. We are losing our minds together and it is fucking amazing. The pit is at my back, I'm ducking the stage divers, Dave is in front of me and every time he moves his sweat falls on my face. I'm pressed up so close to the guy in front of me, if I were a guy I'd be getting accused of rape. My crotch is IN his ass! We are that close. Everyone around me knows every single word and, like with the AFI show in Austin, at points you cannot hear Dave, you can only hear us. We are screaming with all we have. Death metal guys, hardcore kids, girls, guys, white, Mexican, black. We are all one.

I am so happy there are not words for it. The last time I was in this position, with a band I felt this way for, in a venue this size, it was 13 years ago when I was a kid of 22 and seeing Danzig for the first time. I don't feel my age. No time has passed. I am still right there.

So anyway, the band goes into Walk Away. Dave bends over, he is 3 inches from me. He locks eyes with me. My heart stops and all I can think is "Holy hell, he is looking right at me. Something is about to happen."

CUT TO:

October 2nd, 2001, Austin Texas, La Zona Rosa. Davey is standing above me. I cannot physically reach him, his calf is two inches from my hand. We are holding him up and even in fake leather pants I can tell how toned and hard and muscular his legs are.

He looks down and for a good 3 seconds stares right into my eyes. My only thought is "I'm sweating so much I bet he thinks I'm crying. That's why he's looking at me." But I never forgot it. Same eye color, different look, different feel. But I never forgot it.

CUT BACK:

Dave is crouched in front of me, he is singing/screaming/growling and I am screaming along because…I am…it is automatic for the words to pour from my lips in synchronization with his.

He is singing:

"Respect is give and take in my eyes!!! You've scarred everything you are…!!"

It happens.

"You've scarred everything you are…!!"

He leans in and presses his microphone to my lips and I scream with every fiber of my being:

"BUT YOU'LL NEVER SCAR MY PRIDE!!" to complete his lyric. And within a second he has sprang up and is off to sing to the other side of the stage.

There are no words for it. It exists on a level to itself.

I have just sung with my straight edge hero.

Nothing will ever equal that. Ever. Again. Period.

Plenty of times in my life things have happened and I've thought "I can file this in it's own little circle of Hell". But this was the exact opposite. This was my blue heaven. One of the single best five seconds of my life.

According to the 101 Rules of Hardcore, the only reason to go to a hardcore show is to use the guy in front of you as a ladder, get on stage, and steal the mic from the singer so you can sing his song.

I would never do this. I would never do this if I was ten years younger. It is just not in me to do. Guys do this. Guys tackle the singer onstage. I think I saw the dude from XTrip WireX get clothes lined at the Donnybrook show. He ducked it, the guy grabbed his shirt and they both went down, rolling around on the stage. Then the singer popped right up and said something like "Nice try!" and just continued the song like nothing had happened.
Things like this happen to guys.
Things like this do not happen to me.

The rest of the night was a sweaty, screaming, happy blur.
We knew every song, I screamed every song. Even when at times I was positive I was one second away from passing out, I still screamed.
When they went into Hopeless, I screamed out the name of every friend I'd ever lost at the top my lungs. They said they loved me and they just threw me away, ah so many people I could dedicate that song to.

This was the perfect hardcore show. I might as well just stop going now because nothing will ever top it. I would see videos and dvds of live shows and the way the crowd was and the people up front and would always think "God I wanna go to a show like that!".

And Ben on drums…oh god!! He was fucking awesome! In between songs he'd be standing up, egging us on, holding up his sticks in an X. I love that man!

When I got Vendetta and put on the dvd, hearing him talk about being edge…just made me proud to still be here.

Everyone was rubbing Dave's head. I was not that brave but I did wrap my hand around his calf, so…hella!

And I was also not complaining about having his crotch at eye level all night. Nice belt buckle too.

He stopped the show 2 or 3 times because of fighting in the pit. At one point I thought he was just going to walk off stage and stop the show. He kept saying *"Meet me in the parking lot, I've got nothing but time after the show! I'll take you all on!"* Dave is one intense dude. If I were a guy *I* wouldn't fuck with him. He's not the biggest guy in the world, but he is fucking fierce looking!

I just…it was amazing. It was like a dream. It was even better than the night I saw AFI.

Yes, I said it. And I mean it. I didn't think anything could top that night, but this did.

Here are the songs I can remember in no particular order:

We Will Rise
Never Back Down
Back to Zero
Walk Away
Burn
Speak the Truth
New Level (Pantera/Tribute to Dime Bag)
Discipline
Forever
NWD
Hopeless
Slip
Get Sick
Unite

The show ended and I drove home, dazed and happy and got home at 2:45. Axl Rosebush was getting worried, especially since we thought they would go on at 8 or 9 and I'd drive straight home. He was still on the computer so at six am I snuck up to email The girl who called herself Mikey Way and let her know I made it in safe. Went back to ?????????????

Got up at 8 am after four hours of sleep, tasted my first ever Red Bull, drank a latte and went to work to deal with the Spring Break crowds and do inventory. I belched Red Bull and vanilla latte all day.

For the next five years the taste of Red Bull would alwyas remind me of that night.

CHAPTER 20

MY SO CALLED RISE AGAINST LIFE

Yes, AFI was my official "midlife crisis band", however, not even AFI, sings the soundtrack of the last several years of my life like Rise Against has.

I was dragged to my first Rise Against show by Emily. Emily, the suicide girl, quite possibly the hottest girl in Corpus Christi, barely 5'1 and 98 pounds soaking wet, covered in tattoos and with Angelina Jolie's lips. To this day I cannot imagine why a girl who looked like that wanted to hang with me. I had never been to a gig at that little club called The Underground where the disenfranchised youth of Corpus Christi congregated. This was the very cusp of my punk rock midlife crisis and I went in scared to death because I'd heard concerts of this nature were violent.

At this point I was already considering the decision to become straightedge. I was curious but knew little about it. The sum of my knowledge was this: two of the guys in AFI were, and the guy at the mall was. The memory of this guy never leaves me. Like a stray dog with a tennis ball, catching a welcoming scent on the air, then chasing after a passing stranger who never looked down, I chased after him and each year I spent in that fruitless pursuit felt like seven. His friendship I would never win, but he would remain on the outskirts of my life, like the brass ring I reached for again and again only to fall on my face. I would see him that night too, but I didn't know this when Em invited me out.

=+=

It was billed as a hardcore show. I had no idea what hardcore was back then, I just assumed it meant a rough crowd of militant straightedge vegans that would have a sixth sense that I wasn't one of them and chase me out the doors. Rise Against was headlining and an equally unknown band called **Avenged Sevenfold** was opening. I'd never heard of either. Emily wanted me to go and I wanted to get out of the house for the night so it wasn't that hard for her to twist my arm in the matter.

I met her at her apartment which was filth ridden, with drug paraphernalia everywhere, a wall size Misfits poster that took up the entire SIDE of her apartment, and electric guitars propped next to skateboards. As she slipped out of her clothes and into something slinky much to my viewing pleasure, she pointed me to her freezer with a purloined bottle of tropical Schnapps from the liquor store she was working for. Toasting in miniature tea cups I downed the bright blue liquid. I remember it so well, the frost covered bottle, cold in my hand, the electric blueness pouring into what looked like a child's tea party set up. This wasn't the last drink I would take, that would come two months later, yet I remember every detail of the experience.

Suited up in skimpiness, we were off to the races. We hauled ass in Emily's SUV and she sat behind the wheel, dwarfed by it's hugeness and her smallness, joint in hand, careening down the expressway and swerving around orange construction barrels. As we exited into the worst part of town I had ever seen I must have looked uneasy. She turned to me and proudly exclaimed "Don't worry, I know this place! I used to score crack here!"

We walked in and the first person I saw was the straightedge boy, who was taking money at the door. It was a good sign of things to come. It would also mean I would completely ignore Avenged Sevenfold's set in s stupid quest to get his attention long enough to make conversation. But Em was a champ, she stayed with me through the whole thing. In fact, I don't remember having the guts to say a word. She talked to him, I watched him talking to her and twenty feet away M. Shadows was screaming his sexy, tattooed, egotistical lungs out but I was utterly oblivious.

From there we went to the merch booth where Em bought me an Avenged Sevenfold poster that I kept for years on my wall before finally giving it away right on the cusp of actually starting to listen to them.

She also bought me a Rise Against patch that is still on my Dickies bag today though it is nothing more than a mess of black thread.

We wandered over to the PETA booth, watched some gruesome videos, signed up for mail and picked up a cookbook I would later use to make one of the mall kids a vegan birthday cake. Then Emily spied someone she knew and I followed her over, still looking suspiciously through the crowd sure someone was just going to come up and punch me for no apparent reason.

Still following, I watched as she struck up a conversation with this cute guy in glasses. I politely listened in as they talked about how they haven't seen each other since Warped Tour. For the life of me I can't remember what they talked about. I was distracted by a guy that looked like Davey Havok. Their conversation muffled to a drone until the guy looked at his watch and said "Oh crap!! I need to be on stage! I'll talk to after the show!" and it was at that moment I realized Emily had been talking to Joe Principe of Rise Against.

This was our cue as well though there was already too much of a crowd to get near the front. There were maybe one hundred people there and Tim held every one in the palm of his hand. I was amazed. I had never heard them before in my life so I can't tell you the set list but I knew from that time on I wanted to hear more.

=+=

At the end Emily and I waited at the stage to talk to Tim. I had no idea what to say so I just shook his hand and now I wish I had held on a little longer. Emily got a shirt signed and talked to him for a while.

Again I was too preoccupied with the AFI look-alikes in the crowd that I wasn't paying much attention. To this day I wonder if the dude I thought looked like Davey was actually Zacky Vengeance. I'll never know for sure.

Soon enough Joe was with us again and he and Emily were engaged in conversation when he turned to me and said "Did that hurt?" I had NO idea what he was talking about, I was too overwhelmed by his very presence. I actually thought he was pointing past me to the PETA booth and I stupidly sputtered "What KFC is doing to chickens?"

I swear to god when I'm miserable and in need of cheering up sometimes all it takes to make me smile is thinking "Hey, Joe laughed at my joke."

The night drew to an end, Emily went out with the band, and being married, I went home. Next to singing a line with Dave Peters of Throwdown, that first night with Rise Against was the best night of the last ten years of my life.

The next time I would see Rise Against they would be back in Corpus for the last time, opening for Bad Religion. This happened during what I call "The Emo Dave Era". I met Dave because of Rise Against. He was a little emo boy wearing a Rise Against shirt, skipping school at the mall. I stopped him and asked him about it and well that was it, he just kept coming around. I would end up knowing him for five years and eventually hiring him to work for me. By the second time they came to town **Siren Song of The Counterculture** was out and I remember bragging to Dave that if it was any other band I would have just downloaded it, but for them I would actually spend my hard earned money. I remember DRINKING in the songs, trying so hard to memorize all of the tracks before the gig hit.

I remember the second Rise Against gig for many reasons. It was the first gig I went to alone at a time I was in the grip of panic attacks whenever I had to be in wide open spaces by myself. Two of my "mall daughters" met me at the gates and stayed with me the whole night. I remember that. I remember Dave hitting the merch table before me and buying me Rise Against stickers that I regarded like they were jewels and kept them in some special place until I hid them so well I hid them from myself.

Dave and I and the girls were in the front row together, and sadly none of them I am in contact with now. Not only that, but Dave and one of the girls I was up front with would end up working for me and stealing over $1300 from my business during their tenure as my employees. Years from knowing this though we happily stood side by side and sang along for the whole set.

What I remember most about that second gig was standing in front of Joe and when he sang "Single file like soldiers on a mission." I saluted him and he saluted back. Tim was wearing the exact same shirt he wore at the first gig but I was probably the only one to notice it. And when Tim asked "Who was here at our first gig when only 20 people showed up?" I proudly raised my hand. All the memorizing I did was pretty much for naught because I was so excited to be in the front row I damn near forgot every word to every song, but for some reason I knew every word to 1,000 Good Intentions.

The first Rise Against show was in August, I can't tell you the date of the second one. I made my commitment to becoming straightedge sometime between December and January. I don't know the exact date because I was so scared about the whole thing I only told one person. It is only at times like this I remember her: this completely psychotic girl who called herself Belah. She was one of the first mental AFI fans I met but hardly the last. I promise you that 99.9 percent of the AFI fans I met were pathological liars and completely mentally unhinged. It is one of the great unanswered questions of the universe, like how many licks does it take to get to the center of a Tootsie Roll Pop: Are all AFI fans batty because they listen to AFI or were they just batty to begin with and AFI only provided the soundtrack to their insanity? But I digress…Being completely out of her mind, as I would find out later, caused our friendship to expire quickly.

=+=

Even though she was edge two years before me she was hardly supportive and gave me unending hell about it, sure I wouldn't last six months. So only Belah knows the exact date I became edge and she's long gone from my life like almost everyone else from that era. Forgotten. All I know for sure was that I'd been edge several months by the second Rise Against gig at Concrete Street in Corpus.

The second Rise Against gig also brings to mind another phantom of my past: a girl I was close to. I will not mention her name but it was her first night out after being kidnapped and raped. Her parents were druggies and didn't want the cops involved so the guys who did it just got away with it and I'd see them at the mall all the time afterward and I couldn't do shit. It was her and her big sister who met me at the gates and stayed with me all night. I loved those girls…. Again,digressing. From First To Last opened and we spent the whole set talking about how much they looked like AFI.

I ended up leaving the gig early, going to the house of one of them who still lived with his folks, ringing the doorbell and leaving a note in the mail box that said 'YOUR SON RAPES LITTLE GIRLS—just thought you should know'. It didn't really help anything but it made me feel better.

During this mindlessly courageous time I was blinded by my commitment. I jumped into being edge with a fervor reserved for things like joining the Hari Krishnas or Jehovah's Witnesses. It was a complete makeover of every idea I'd ever held. I didn't know a great deal but once I found it, I knew it was all I had been looking for. The only other person I actually knew who was edge was the straightedge boy, who now had become god-like in my mind. He was the first face of straightedge for me, the ideal, the standard, the one thing I felt I had to live up to. Sadly, by this time he was long gone, moving away from the mall where we worked and on to better things. This fact only drove me forward in a Holy Grail level quest to find him. When he was there I was terrified of speaking to him and then when he wasn't I kicked myself for not having the courage. I was sure that if I did make my way to him, he could impart some knowledge, some advice that would make my whole solitary experience make sense. The soundtrack of that quest was **Blood to Bleed**:

CHAPTER 21

Within weeks of each other three amazing things happened: "The generic scene girl from Austin", my best friend Dionysus, and I went to Warped Tour to see AFI and in the process saw Rise Against as well. Then The Sufferer and the Witness came out, and at the same time The girl who loved Jade Puget and The generic scene girl from Austin came to visit me in Corpus for quite possibly the most idyllic summer of my life.

It was that summer we saw Rise Against for the third time. At that Warped Tour again we were in front of Joe, and again when Tim sang *"Single file like soldiers on a mission..."* we saluted Joe and he saluted us back and it was like a little piece of heaven fell to earth, the moment was so perfect. The set was short because it was Warped Tour but we didn't care. We were together, we loved each other and we sang along with every song we knew.

Sufferer and Witness came out in July right in time for Warped Tour and the girls coming down for a visit. I remember this so well because I had a cd of the straightedge boy's band and it seemed so important for me to play it for "The girl who loved Jade Puget" and "The generic scene girl from Austin". Do you remember that line in **The Lost Boys**: *"Now you know what we are, now you know what you are."* ? That was how it felt for me, this romanticized notion that my edge was not my own and it was all owing and belonged to someone else. I wanted to be able to trace it like a family tree to say, if I had not met him I would not have found out about AFI, I would not have made my commitment, we would have never met, so therefore the life and friendship we have shared has all traced back to THIS.

Well, they weren't all that impressed. I have a very clear memory of us being outside the Sonic Drive In and the girl who loved Jade Puget asking me "Please turn that noise off and put in something else." That something else was the **The Sufferer And The Witness** and it stayed in the player for the rest of the trip.

=+=

Ready To Fall was the song that defined the next year, much later, that I made my edge my own. In my journey I had looked to so many others for advice or reassurance or validation. I did this because I didn't believe in myself. I thought I was weak and sought in others what would make me strong. Sometimes I received it, like messages sent back and forth with the guys in Throwdown and the near religious experience of seeing them live all the times I have, of singing a line with Dave, shaking his hand.

Most of the time though, my search was in vain.

I remember very clearly seeking out help online. One guy told me I would never know who I was until I went to a hardcore show. This wasn't exactly bad advice, hardcore shows had the most amazing energy flowing through them and it did feel good to be surrounded by likeminded people. The only thing I really learned about myself through going to hardcore shows was that if God had wanted me to hardcore dance, He would not have given me boobs.

There was another guy who told me only the most insecure person would EVER wear a straightedge shirt out in public and if you were sincere about it, you'd keep it to yourself. I thought that guy was nuts. The whole POINT of being edge to me was proving I was not like the idiots around me.

I asked another guy what to do if I was tempted to drink again and he told me if I was tempted I was never really straightedge to begin with and I should just do the scene a favor and kill myself already. Then there were the kids that thought I was just the bees' knees and were coming to ME for advice. I had no idea what to tell these kids, but I wasn't about to tell them not to wear sXe gear or kill themselves. Because of my own search for answers I refused to turn any kid away. One day they were telling me I was their hero and begging for advice, the next they were telling me I was out of my mind and to get lost. It took a good four years before I learned not to believe them in either case.

=+=

Right in the middle of this I had the good fortune to meet a guy named Chris Streiegel, aka Chris X from Philly. He neither worshipped nor ignored me. He was simply THERE. I have the most vivid memory of this one morning. I had the same dream about the straightedge boy only this time I stepped out and stopped him and asked him if the hormones levels in milk made people more aggressive the way steroids did and asked if I should stop drinking it. Why this popped into my head I will never know. As usual the alarm rang before the blurry form opened his mouth and imparted wisdom. I woke up at 5 am and suddenly HAD to know the answer to the question. It happened that Chris X was up too. I contacted him and he took the time out of his morning to discuss this with me completely out of the blue. I don't know why this sticks out in my memory but it does: Him being up at five am and taking an hour out of his morning to answer some moronic question from a girl he didn't know and being so nice about it.

He is still edge, we are still friends and he is still there when I need him. He is the exception to the rule. Friends fell away and I remained steadfast, yet alone.

Slowly though there came the time when I realized I needed to look no further than in the mirror. It wasn't like this was a new thing. I was told this many times and yet I never believed it. Right about this time Rise Against released **Ready To Fall**: They had a line about turning from the heights once loved and running away like hell.

The heights I once loved were ego driven, the compulsion to wear a straightedge shirt every day and X's for every gig and dare anyone to tell me otherwise. It was that romanticized notion of my edge,—that it hadn't been mine and all I was, was owed to someone else. It was as if I believed someone had physically stood between me and a fridge full of alcohol that first year and kept me from it. Or that someone had been there to comfort me when my husband was drunk or in a bad mood and was calling me names or throwing me around because I dared come home with a book of Marxist writing or simply did not shut up and go along or renounce my beliefs. I healed myself, I comforted myself and I did almost all of it completely alone. It was slow in dawning but it finally came to me that I was the only one I had to inspire or impress, and my own approval was all I needed. This revelation was scored by every track on **Sufferer and Witness**.

=+=

The fourth time I saw Rise Against, I met the generic scene girl from Austin in Austin to see them at Stubbs'. Stubbs' BBQ is a grand place to see any band because if you get there early enough, you can have lunch on the balcony while watching the band's sound check. We found this out the first time we went there, seeing The Rollins Band open up for X. Going to the Rise Against show I told myself "It's not big deal, I've seen them three times before, I'm just going to kick back and eat and enjoy the sound check" but as soon as Tim and Joe took the stage I could barely consume a thing I was so overwhelmed.

As we waited in line after lunch for the doors to reopen, I met that generic scene girl from Austin's brother Jordan who is, wildly enough, still my friend. Jordan, my straightedge brother and one of my closest friends. He hovers on the edges of my life, always there with a kind word whether I actually deserved it or not. He is the only good thing to come out of my friendship with The generic scene girl from Austin.

Evergreen Terrace opened that show and we were right in front of the guy in the Straightedge Soldier t-shirt and that and a brilliant cover of "Mad World" was all I remembered of their set. Circa Survive came on next and the generic scene girl from Austin and I took turns booing them and flipping them off. Not that they were necessarily bad, but we were in no mood to entertain the mopey emo set at that point. Soon we were all piled together up front, again in front of Joe. I didn't get to salute him at that gig. the generic scene girl from Austin's arms were too tightly around me. The girl from Austin, her girlfriend Grace, Jordan and my husband were tangled in a sea of arms, so tightly that I wasn't sure of whose hand I was holding most of the night.

Though by that time I was perfectly comfortable in my commitment, **Blood to Bleed** still only reminded me of one person and the girl from Austin knew this. I felt she understood me then, I felt she was one of the very few who knew me best. Beside me was my husband, but in my heart was a dream of someone else, of someone who shared my commitment and my ideals, a dream of an idea more than a person, the perfect guy/relationship/life I would never have.

Two months later I would find out my husband was seeing a girl from work that had got him hooked on dope. Two months later he would come to where I worked and attack me in front of multiple witnesses and when called, the police would do nothing. Two months later I would sit sobbing in the back of a police car because I was too afraid to go into my own apartment and get my things. When responding to my call the enormous officer would glare down at me and say "Why are you afraid to walk in your own home? Are you on drugs or are you just retarded?" Instead of accompanying me inside to get my things they would search me for drugs.

Two months later I would realize why Henry Rollins hated cops so much. Two months later. after ten years together, I would leave my husband.

I did not know any of this then.

All I knew was that in that instant my heart was bleeding inside of me for want of some friendship I would never have, the one thing I believed would make my life complete. It was that friendship, that idea of a person, of perfection, of everything I wanted myself and my life to be, that seemed like the holy grail of the second part of my life. Looking back, maybe it held value only because it was unobtainable. I had not yet learned to find it in myself so I sought it so furiously in a stranger. So, with the ridiculously angelic vision of the first straightedge boy I ever met in my head, and my unfaithful husband beside me, in that crowd at Stubb's, Rise Against tore into **Blood To Bleed**.

It was our first time to hear it live together as they had not played it at Warped Tour. The generic scene girl from Austin looked down at me, wrapped her arms around me and held me tight because she knew exactly who I was thinking of and why. As she held on to me with one hand and ran a hand through my hair, we both screamed out those lyrics that had haunted me and driven me on for years.

=+=

And just like I was blind to what was about to erupt with my husband I was just as blind to time bomb ticking inside of the girl from Austin that would turn her into a complete stranger the next time we met, at the very same place it would turn out. Had I known that this was the last time she would hold my hand and sing with me and look down on me with love and empathy in her eyes, I would not have wasted my sorrow in grieving for a friendship that never was and instead would have known to grieve for the real friendship I was losing. I should have grieved for hers, but in retrospect, it was no more real than the idea of the one I chased after so fruitlessly.

And the strange footnote to that day, that time, that moment of hope and loss and all that was to come is this: Even though his friendship I never actually earned, in his status of a wise, polite stranger, that straightedge boy I never really knew was far more civil than the generic scene girl from Austin. His responses, however short they were, however long it took to get them, were genuine. It is such a small thing, his honesty, yet it is more than I can say for ninety percent of the people I've known in the last several years.

Another song we sang together that night was **Prayer of the Refugee**. I had no idea then but that song was about to describe my life.

The split with my husband was brutal. First I had to deal with police that didn't care, who told me at one point "Well, if he tries to kill you, call us back, otherwise there's nothing we can do. He's your husband and he has the same right to live here as you do." Thanks to the police not doing anything, I was thrown out of the apartment I had paid for, for ten years. The battered women's shelter was full and I would have found myself homeless had it not been for my friend Ylliona. Suddenly I was having to start from scratch and then, upon finding a place, having to pack up ten years worth of my life and move it all by myself.

My husband, before going to live with his mother, ran our car until the brakes were out and he was driving on two flat tires, then left it at the ER, unlocked with our big screen tv in the back seat, apparently en route to the pawn shop. He checked himself in and when he called me for sympathy I took the car and the apartment back, both wrecked. By this time I had already given a vacate notice to the complex of the apartment where he had punched holes in every wall and turned in into an overflowing trash heap. I left it behind with a good chunk of myself and found a cozy if expensive place elsewhere.

Every day I worked until the afternoon, went home and packed until 2 am, fell asleep until 5 am and then got up and did it all again. Then once I was packed I had to move it all. I can't remember why I didn't ask for help but I moved it all alone except for the bed, entertainment center and tv.

This was such a strange time. There was no way to hide what was going on: my husband came to where I worked and jumped me in front of everyone there, I had to tell my boss "My husband kicked me out and I'm homeless at the moment, could I possibly get my check a day or two early to put a deposit down on an apartment?" and I had to own up to the fact that I was straightedge and my husband was a heroin addict.

This made my life suddenly seem a really bad B movie. There was nothing to do but go on. I would have asked myself "What would that straightedge guy do in this situation?" if I'd had any idea. Instead I asked "What would Dave Peters of Throwdown do?" and of course the obvious answer was "punch something". As much as I wanted to, I couldn't do that. However, I knew for sure what he *wouldn't* do and that was curl up in a ball and cry. So I didn't do that either. It was a such horrible time and yet when I look back all I remember is my own strength and the exhilaration I felt when I finally left.

Ylliona, my Wiccan friend from the nights I hung out at the tea room and Di the one AFI fan I knew in person, swore I looked great, like I had suddenly gotten 10 years younger. They said I was glowing, but unless I had come in contact with radium I certainly didn't see how. I remember thinking "Well hell, maybe the Socialists were right. Maybe 16 hour days are the way to salvation."

CHAPTER 22

As I came into my own power, Chris, the straightedge boy who had loomed so god-like over the first years of my commitment shrank back down to human size. Deep down I still hoped that if he was to know of all I had gone through he would be a little proud of me for surviving with my integrity intact. But if he didn't, well that was okay too. Survive I did, survive I continue to.

When I had my own place and my own life again, to celebrate I bought myself a Christmas present: a tattoo of a sparrow carrying brass knuckles in her beak. It reminded me of this lyric that had been echoing in my head the whole time:

I enjoyed more than six months of solitude in my cozy little apartment on Airline. I filled my weekends with walks on the beach, solitary shopping excursions for meatless dinners, and nights were spent at the House of Rock and the Underground watching bands, enjoying the freedom of staying out without getting yelled at or called names. I spent Christmas alone on Ylliona's floor stuffing myself with processed cheese balls and watching movies. It was my first UnChristmas. The Jehovah's Witnesses would have been proud!

But I am flawed and cowed and crippled by the Christian concept of forgiveness. And by the time I would be seeing Rise Against again, my husband would be back by my side. In West Texas his mom had ran him through the MHMR system, let them start him on 7 different drugs,— including three different tranquilizers and pills for hallucinations and seizures, which he never once had,—used him to get on welfare, disability, and Medicare. Once he's served the purpose, she called a friend in the sheriff's department and had him pulled from her house, drugged out of his mind on meds at the time, and stuck on a bus to Corpus Christi. The Glasscock County Sherriffs' Department called me at work to TELL me "Your husband is on a bus to Corpus, he'll be there at two AM. He's your responsibility now." On the bus, because of his state of stupor, he was robbed of everything but his clothes and as much as I wanted to just shove him into the closest homeless shelter, I couldn't. Had it been me, as unlikely as that would be, I would want someone to have compassion.

I took him in. At first it was easy. Thanks to the drugs he was sleeping 18 hours a day. Finally I started to investigate what they had him on, what he could do without and how to get him back to normal. I'm not sure how I did it, but I weened him off of every drug he was on. At first it was out of necessity since I was making too much money for him to stay on state sponsored help and he'd have run out eventually. Looking back though, had he sustained that amount of drug intake for long he would have probably died.

So he was back for good and conversely the generic scene girl from Austin and the girl who loved Jade Puget and nearly every other friend I had at the time would have turned their backs on me and flocked to other, cooler individuals. All those kids that convinced me they would have killed themselves, starved themselves, cut themselves to shreds, OD'ed, etc had they not met me, who all imposed their problems and lives on mine for five years or more and took up every spare moment of my time and every inch of my heart all turned 18 at once. In turning 18 they realized they knew it all and I was no longer worth their time.

=+=

My husband and I are still together, but all those friends are long gone. I wish I could say he gave up all his demons, but he didn't. He simply traded the big ones for a myriad of lesser evils. He will never be straightedge. I love him though because for better or worse he was always there, he was mostly honest, when he was sober anyway, and he never gave up on me. I did not want to give up on him.

Though he claims to be proud of me, to this day he is convinced, utterly falsely, I am hiding some secret affair with the straightedge boy from years ago. I sat him down one day and asked "Do you get that we are straightedge? Do you get that in being straightedge we could not possibly cheat on our significant others and remain straightedge? Do you get that no matter how much he influenced me I barely knew him and he barely gave me the time of day? Do you get that what you are accusing me of is utterly impossible?".

Despite his insistence on this, the idea doesn't bother him enough for him to give up his addictions and become edge himself. He no longer asks me to change and he is no longer violent, thank god. I no longer ask him to change, though I pray every day he will. We coexist, which doesn't keep me from dreaming of some nice sXe man who shares my ideals. But I think of it much like I imagine walking the streets of Paris, knowing it will never actually happen. I love him, he loves me, we will never agree on how he chooses to abuse his body. It is something I have learned to accept. He has been with me, been there for me, when I did not have one single other friend on this earth.

=+=

Things in my life settled down for a bit as we prepared to see the boys again at Stubbs' BBQ. Through myspace I found my friend Linda that I had not spoken to in fifteen years. As we sat on the balcony at Stubbs' I kept one eye on the stage and the other on the door waiting to see her again.

When she walked through the doors it was like the last fifteen years never even happened and instantly we picked up right where we left off and again were tearing through Austin with her at the wheel like we had so many times in the past. Because of this joyful reunion I was not first in line when the doors opened, I was buying rainbow necklaces in the gay shops in town and snickering over whether the guy behind the counter was flirting with my husband or not.

That was a strange memory for me, being in the very back of the audience for once, singing alone as Axl Rosebush sat on a rock and read a Robert Jordan novel. I was happy to be there, the music was incredible, but the feeling was all wrong. I was isolated and alone, in the back row with my fist raised and Axl Rosebush tugging at my arm every other song asking "What song is this? Do I know this one?". I wondered if The generic scene girl from Austin was there in the front row, holding on to someone else and convincing them she would have killed herself if they hadn't come into her life. I imagined others in the front row, in our place, saluting Joe, singing our songs while I was the interloper that did not belong anymore.

We walked out of the sold out show before the encore, a long drive home facing us. Axl Rosebush never lets me stay for the encores. He always wants to hit the road. As we walked to the car, with Worth Dying For wafting through the air above us, I blew a kiss to the wind and told The generic scene girl from Austin goodbye.

It was the lyrics of Rise Against that echoed in my head when I sat down to read the words of Marx and Lenin for the first time as a whole other world opened up for me. It was Rise Against that drove me on as I worked sixty hour weeks.

Their lyrics saw me through every major event of the last several years of my life. Appeal to Reason was released in the Fall of 2008 and though the year found me miserably poor and unemployed, I still bought it the day it came out. It was on my mp3 player and as I sat in the welfare office applying for food stamps I would hear the lyrics *"Despite these petty fortunes we still can't afford a life…"* for the first time and I would pause a moment just for the whole zeitgeist effect of it.

=+=

For Christmas of 2008 I received an email from The generic scene girl from Austin after a year and a half of ignoring my every attempt at contacting her. I had tried everything, even terribly childish measures to get some kind of reaction but every letter—first polite, then angry, then groveling—every call, email, and package was met with silence. A year and a half passed and then I got the email saying "I got the new Rise Against and it made me realize how much I loved and missed you and loved AFI and I want to be friends again. I know you can't forgive me but can we be friends again? There's this song on that new Rise Against that reminds me of you."

True to the bond we had once held there was certainly a song on the new Rise Against that reminded me of us too:

This was exactly what happened the last time we saw each other when she turned up her nose and pretended not to know who I was, just a week after sending me a letter saying how much she loved me. This led to the year plus of her not speaking to and ignoring all attempts at contact I made, even the immature ones.

But too much time had passed and although that Christian weakness crippled me so with my husband, for once I stood strong and had no trouble in keeping the door to my heart shut. I told her not to contact me again.

That doesn't mean that my mind does not still light to her like a bee to a flower, the years we were friends, that feeling of love and camaraderie and the bond I imagined we had. The last three Rise Against albums play the soundtrack of our friendship whenever I turn them on. When I play **Appeal to Reason** I wonder if this song reminds her of me:

If I close my eyes I am there again in that Port Aransas condo, the night we met face to face after talking online for so long. We are huddled together in the bedroom sharing the earphones of a cd player listening to Placebo's Sleeping With Ghosts. I am pulling down the zipper of my boot and showing her three freshly razored X's cut into my ankle, the blood still stuck to a wad of tissue pressed between my sock and skin. She is crying and wrapping her arms around me and telling me she understands everything and that someday she will show me her scars too.

She never did show me her scars. I wonder now if she even had any. There are lots of songs that transport me back then when she was my world. But now I know nothing about her nor anyone else I knew then was real and I wonder if that song ever reminds her of me and the way she led me to believe I was her lifeline, right up until the moment she cut me off and forgot me like a favorite toy after adolescence destroys the need for such playthings.

This is the music that accompanied my feet hitting the pavement of park sidewalks and treadmills, it is the melodies that buoyed me through endless work weeks and settled into the recesses of my heart in times of quiet contemplation.

As I read words written years ago by writers we were never allowed to study in school, it is the soundtrack that played in my mind when those concepts began to make sense. When I read the words of John Reed, Marx, Lenin and John Maynard Keynes, it was the lyrics of Tim McIlrath that I heard in my head.

CHAPTER 23

I look back at many things and laugh. I remember when I was first looking for straightedge shirts I came upon one that said SUPPORT LEFTIST HARDCORE. I had no earthly idea what it meant and was way too scared to ask anyone. Now I can quote Trotsky. When I first turned edge I stopped eating meat for several months until my husband found out and started calling me a Communist. At the time it seemed like the worst thing in the world to be called. He still calls me a Communist but now with laughable results. I'll cock my head, say something to him in Russian, he'll mumble under his breath 'Yeah you only say that because you've had sex with the entire Communist party!", I'll roll my eyes and we go back to living: together and yet at opposite ends of the galaxy. I love him. I cannot save him. He will never be straight edge and I will spend the rest of my life mourning that fact. I will compose daydreams in my head of a perfect man, exactly like him except poison free, and maybe with a cute pair of Buddy Holly style glasses. The world will go on. We fall in love, we fall out of love, we fall in love all over again and I am sure we will stay together until the day we die.

I had always loved the way the Russian alphabet looked, even before my romance with Communism. Shortly after we were married I got a tramp stamp with his initials in Russian letters on the inside of what was once the logo for the ECW wrestler Taz.

He used to jokingly claim it actually meant "Welcome aboard, Comrade." I would just laugh and life would go on.

In the great Holy Grail of a search for wisdom that I thought could only come from the first straightedge boy I knew, I had one great fear: what if I found him again and he was no longer edge? I was terrified of this, sure that if he fell I would too, that if that touchstone was gone, all would be lost. This no longer worries me. I would be sad if it happened, but it would not affect my journey nor cause me to stumble because I have found my own way. It was hard way full of work, trial and error and pure blind luck. Maybe it would have been easier if things had gone differently and yet it is all mine and no one else's.

Every hero I have had was really anything but. They were all fallible, as much as I thought they were like me, they weren't. They never asked to be my heroes and I worshipped them as gods anyway so their mortality was my own faith's fault.

Being straightedge and being middle aged is a strange and lonely journey. It is like being the last of a dying breed, waiting on its own extinction. It is like being on Logan's Run. I am X'ed up and cast out and though many surround me and some still claim to look up to me, I am utterly alone in my convictions because no one's story is the same as mine.

Rise Against is the music that scores ALL of this in my memory.

It is the sound of hope and loss, of new directions and ideas, of the brass ring becoming just another small cog in the great, silent machinations of my soul. It is the music of discovering that the strength of the world lies inside my own heart. It is the sound of me walking away from what I loved, it is the joyous noise of friends you're certain is lost forever coming back to you.

CHAPTER 24

By the end of my seventh year at the mall, the romance was gone, the monotony had set in and I was fed up with answering the same questions every single day. Still, good things were happening for a while. I hired a girl named Laura, and though I didn't know it at the time, she would quickly become my running buddy.

I have always been so sure that if everyone loved the things I loved and lived life as I did, the world would be an incredible and tolerant place. I have always been elitist that way, having an only child's sense of manifest destiny and entitlement. For once though I was really able to convince someone the music I loved was tops. Soon Laura was accompanying me to every show of my latest obsession: Americana / Texas music. We were regular fixtures at the Executive Surf Club, so much so that when I met Jack Ingram he swore he had seen me before though I can't remember ever going to one of his gigs. We attended so many shows for and were such rabid fans of the western swing, rockabilly outfit, The Derailers, that when they came to the stage, they stopped and shook our hands or tipped their cowboy hats to us.

It was a great time to be alive. I used to go to their gigs as much for the muisc as to watch the swing dancers, and one boy in particular. I had no idea who he was, but he was the best dancer I had ever seen. Then one day at the mall, the local country station, KFTX had a promotion with the Girl Scouts because it was time to sell cookies again. I was hawking my wares when two guys came up, on their way to the remote broadcast to get a sample. I stared in disbelief as the one and only king of swing stood before me. I introduced myself, he introduced himself and it turned out he was a deejay for the KFTX. His name was Chris O'Brien.

From that day forward when Laura and I made our attendance known at all the local country gigs, we would always run into Chris and his dance partner. One night before I became straightedge we all did shots with the Derailers at a Christmas show at the VFW Hall in Annaville. It might not sound like much from the outside but it was some of the greatest times of my life, times I never forgot that my mind goes back to again and again. He asked me to dance once, Chris. He wouldn't remember it, he was too drunk, but I'll never forget it as long as I live. He inclined his head, placed one hand over my left ear and whispered into my right "Do you swing, baby?" and I think my very soul left my body from the thrill of it. For the record, I can't dance. I can't chew gum and walk at the same time and I wanted to say yes with every fiber in my being but I said no. I look back on that as one of my only regrets in life. I cannot think of Chris without thinking of the Derailers, nor can I think of the Derailers or hear their music without thinking of Chris. It is my warm, happy place every bit as much as the front of the stage at the White Rabbit in San Antonio where I sang a line with Dave Peters.

I used to wonder why I enjoyed Jay Baruchel's movies (Fanboys, She's Outta My League, The Sorcerer's Apprentice) and why I thought he was just so damn cute. It finally hit me: He reminded me of Chris O'Brien.

=+=

During my time as a general manager of my own little dominion at the mall, the best thing, aside from the kids, was getting to make my own schedule. Because of this I was able to visit my sister Toni whenever she flew back home from the Virgin Islands. I have other family that I will not speak of, but Toni was the only person who ever loved me unconditionally—even when I blurted out that I liked girls and embarrassed the both of us horribly in front of her best friend. She has always helped me when I needed it. We are technically half sisters, having the same father but different mothers, but I think of her as my one and only real sister. When I lived in Big Spring, she lived in Dallas and then the Virgin Islands. When I moved to Corpus, she moved back to Big Spring and we were still miles and hours apart. Still, once every year or so she would pay to fly me back home to meet her and spend some time in West Texas, where the dry heat was a welcome relief from the South Texas humidity and time slowed down to a crawl.

Each visit I would always make a point to contact my friend Kay Courtright. By this time she had married a man named Charles and just like she had nick named me Joseph she had nick named him Charles Atlas. She seemed truly happy for the first time since we met and I was happy for her. I was standing in my sister's kitchen one day in July. I had just called work to make sure the stand had not been burned down by the teenage employees I'd left in charge. I dialed Kay's number and Charles Atlas answered.

"Can I speak to Kay?"
"Who is this?" he demanded.
"Joseph."
"Who?!"
"Joseph. Joey? Her son? Remember we had lunch last year at La Posada?"
"Joey…" His voice trailed off. "Kay's dead."
"WHAT?! When? Why didn't someone call me?! What happened?!"

Kay had been battling Lupus the entire time I had known her but it never seemed to be that bad. Things had apparently changed in the years since I had left home and Kay had died due to complications from the disease. It never occurred to Charlies, probably too consumed with his own grief, to call or write and let me know. And so the last person I latched on to as a mother passed from my life and on to the next.

When I was in high school I thought it was a cute thing to do to call the mothers of my friends "Mom" since I didn't have one. After Kay died I never called anyone Mom ever again.

=+=

132

Much like the day at the theater when I realized that popcorn and free movie passes weren't paying my rent, there came a time when I realized my sanity was worth more than thirteen dollars an hour. Boy, was I an idiot to quit a job that paid that wage. NO ONE in Corpus got paid dough like that unless they were on staff at a refinery. I got to the point where I could not take it anymore. I could not take working sixty hours a week form Halloween until New Years and never once being told thank you or good job. I could not continue to stomach the same stalkers coming by to harass me every single day. After nearly ten years of dealing with the same people and answering the same questions every single day I was over my limit of tolerance and had had enough.

Out of all the mall walkers there was one couple I actually thought of as my own surrogate parents. Zeki and Hayat came from Iraq, fleeing the regime of Sadaam Hussein. They both held prominent positions in the government and were paragons of education and culture. They fled to Indiana where they were both professors at one of the universities then came to Corpus to retire.

Hayat would pass by every day and tease me about being the only shop clerk who actually read during her down time instead of staring at the walls or doing her nails. It started out like that, but then she began to critique the books I was reading and would challenge me to read better, deeper, more literary works. When I told her I held a degree in Business and a degree in English she was appalled. Why was I wasting my life selling snacks to inbred morons? Okay, maybe those are my words, not hers, but that was the gist of what she lectured me about.

"What do you want to do?" she asked me and in my heart of hearts I knew one thing: I wanted to teach English. I wanted to teach the types of kids who flocked to my stand. I wanted to teach the types of kids I tried to mentor. I wanted to teach kids because I would never have any of my own. I wanted to teach kids because no one in Corpus stayed in school past the ninth grade and I felt I was their last grasp at the golden ring that was an educated, literary mind. At Hayat's urging I set about to find a way to make this happen.

=+=

Before I leave the subject of the mall, I want to share one last memory. Christmas was a fun time but it was grueling. No matter how much we sold, our owner was never happy. I worked sixty hours a week and ended up getting sick every single year. Each day before Christmas Eve the mall would be open until midnight or later and then it would open back up at seven am the next morning. So I would work until one or two in the morning, go home, get a couple of hours of sleep and be back at six am to start getting ready to open. One year I was just dragging myself in at six in the morning, exhausted beyond words and still half asleep. Someone I did not know approached me, and at first I thought she was a customer and I was preparing my speech about how we weren't open yet but give me five minutes to get the register up and what not. She stopped me and offered me a plate of muffins. I was floored. I'm not sure where she worked but I know she was a mall employee, heading to open her store. I smiled, took a muffin and thanked her. I never saw her again, but it is the simplest most unselfish acts of kindness that never leave my memory. I never forgot her.

=+=

I will freely admit that I am gullible. It's not as bad as it used to be, but I fear I will never lose this trusting nature until the day I die, no matter what a sarcastic, jaded, elitist bitch I pretend to be in real life. I have wrongly believed in family members, boys, girls, politicians and spiritual leaders. However, education remained my true religion. Educators were above reproach, they were blameless, free of guile, and would never lead one astray.

I believed this right up until the day I completed my alternative teaching certification program by scoring the third highest score in a class of forty two and realized I had ditched my good paying mall job for nothing, there were no teaching jobs to be had and I was facing a future of unemployment. It was that day that I learned their promise of a ninety five percent placement rate actually meant "Good luck, moron, thanks for the tuition and don't let the door hit you on the way out."

They put a great face on everything. Potential students had to pass an entrance exam, write a letter of application, send out a sizable application fee and pass a panel interview. I did all this was was as accepted as part of forty two or so new students, I was the only one in my field of middle school English, which I naively thought meant I had no competition.

In order to attend every day for eight hours a day and go home at night to do projects, I would not have time to put in as many hours as I had at the mall. I called our owner and explained to him that I had put in nine years of faithful service during which time I took our average monthly profits from six thousand dollars a month to eighteen thousand dollars a month. I told him I would be glad to stay on until I got a teaching job but instead of working mornings, I could only work nights and weekends. The owner told me he no longer needed my services as a manager, busted me down to a regular employee and hired to replace me and be my boss, a girl I had fired two years earlier for sitting on her cell phone all day and refusing to wait on customers. She was quite a nice looking girl, but she was a shitty employee with no customer service skills and no education and she was given MY job.

I wrote the owner a nine page email and quit. My usurper lasted six months before she drove the stand out of business. I had made it work for nine years, I had made it successful for nine years and in six months she bankrupted the place.

I worked diligently in my classes and for the first time in many years I had friends my own age. I met Lein who was Vietnamese, Dee who was Croatian, and Mel who was Filipina. For one year we were inseparable as we set out to conquer the world of education. We were told there were more than enough teaching jobs and that by virtue of our participation in "the" premiere certification program, we could pretty much go out and take any teaching job we wanted.

That year came to be known as Mission Impossible.

=+=

In the summer of 08 Mel, Lein, Dee, and I set out to put our newly minted teaching certifications to good use, We were all excited and full of hope. We went out every day together, hitting every school, dropping off our resumes, calling each other if we saw something come up in the other person's field. These all day excursions were made fun because we were such good friends and could find humor in anything. However, the weeks went slowly by and we remained unemployed.

We went on interviews that went well and we never got the job, we went on interviews that went horribly, we responded to job offers asking for one thing and once we actually got the interview, they asked for or offered something else . We drove all over South Texas in the heat, getting eaten alive by mosquitoes. None of us were working. The women whose husband's made the most money provided the transportation and gas. We drove as far as 60 miles away and on one job called and *begged* for an interview, was told we would be interviewed, packed up, drove 45 minutes out of town, got to the school and was told "Oh I'm sorry, someone gave you the wrong information, that position was already filled."

By the end of the summer our spirits were tanking.

We were receiving no help or support from the program and mentors that had promised to stand by us and help us get jobs. I guess what they really meant to say was "We'll back you until your tuition check clears and then you are on your own." I complained so much and so loudly about this to anyone who would listen, sending rambling, disgruntled emails to mentors and students alike, I was brought up in disciplinary hearing. Apparently you were not allowed as a paying student to complain about the 95 % placement rate that was touted in order to get me to enroll and pay my fees.

As I went through the program however, one third of the students had dropped out and there wasn't even a 95% placement rate in the rest that remained. The program was hyped as being the best in the area. Once we started going on interviews though, we found out nobody cared.

Upon completion, even with the third highest state exam grade in the class, I was still unemployed. When I complained to my instructors, (who—at the first of the course BEFORE they took all our money— were the biggest gung ho cheerleaders around) I was utterly ignored.

This made me complain MORE and to everyone who would listen, which was ignored until I was sending out emails clearly reflecting my status of being on the verge of a nervous breakdown. But complaining about this to whoever would listen was apparently a no-no and, like I said, I ended up having to pay a lawyer to sit in the meeting with me just so they wouldn't try to take advantage of me further (ie kick me out when I had done nothing wrong and violated no rules). As soon as they saw I had legal counsel, the meeting was no longer called disciplinary and I was told the reason all my emails were ignored because I never asked a specific question!!! Apparently "Please tell me what I am doing wrong in these interviews, I am at the end of my rope!!" was not specific enough.

In the end I paid a friend who was a lawyer $250 to come sit with me at the hearing and look heavy—hell I could have paid some bum off the street $25 and probably gotten the same effect and they took everything back and said because I didn't get a job this year my fee payments and tuition payments (which I had foolishly paid in advance) would carry over to the next year without me having to register all over again.

=+=

We had dubbed the summer MISSION IMPOSSIBLE. As we drove through the area that I ended up working at for what I'll call "redneck electronics"(which I will explain about later) , an area known for it's hookers, Dee put forth that she could procure a job as a prostitute faster AND make more money than she could as a teacher. Dee was beautiful and she had a point. But she was also the first of us to get a job. But the fact that she scored a PERFECT score on the state exam for teaching higher Math was still only good enough to get her a job at one of the worst, most violent, low income schools in the ares. Though she was the first of us to get a job it still came at the LAST minute in 08, after 4 months of exhausting leg work.

I should have known what was to come early on. I should have smelled the rat that was the lie of an easy b\path to finding a job. During the second week of class a superintendent from the highest paying school district came and made a presentation. She talked about how she would always give "our" candidates the interview first if more than one application was on her desk. We were the cream of the crop, she loved our organization and program and we would always have a place working for her. She really laid it on with the rah-rah pep talk. Three months later a position opened up at her junior high in my field. I was ecstatic. This was my ticket to the big leagues. I was the only candidate in the program teaching this subject at this level, I had passed my state exam with flying colors. I was a sure thing, baby!

I called and asked for an interview. And called, and called and called. I never even got to speak to anyone other than the secretary. The superintendent refused to speak to me. I tried for three years and never once got the a call back, much less an interview. It may have been a good thing that I did not speak to the old shrew superintendent. A fellow classmate approached her at a job fair, introduced herself from our program and asked about employment to which the old beast replied "Why on earth would I hire you? You have no student teaching experience!" and walked away.

I went on one particular interview in Alice, Texas. Alice is two hours away and it took all the money I had in the bank at the time to get gas. They invited me out, I drove all the way out there and then…I guess they were expecting a guy or something but when the interviewer actually SAW me her whole attitude changed and she was like "Well we don't hire people that use Microsoft when we use Mac's because Microsoft people can't make the switch over". What this had to do with my talents as an English teacher I have no idea. Then she said "How do I know you're not going to just use us to get your first year out of the way and then go to another school once you get your permanent certification?". Yes, I would choose willingly to drive two hours each way every day only to leave the first chance I got. This just seemed counterproductive to me. THEN after interviewing me for an English position, knowing I was only certified for English she closes the interview by saying "Well we were REALLY only looking for a Social Studies teacher anyway. Can you teach Social Studies?" It was truly as if I had to know some secret Masonic code in order to get a job. It was almost as if they were making up reasons not to hire me, though I have no idea why.

CHAPTER 25

When I quit the job at the mall I realized we would have to tighten our belts. We had just taken over payments of a new car after two major accidents, neither our fault, that totaled our last two vehicles. I gave the car up to save money and took the bus everywhere. My husband lived within walking distance of his job and I figured I was young and healthy enough to walk wherever I needed to go until I could get a good teaching job and buy another car. Christmas of 2008 found me with no car, no job and not prospects.

I then spent nearly two years of being unemployed, being turned down for food stamps and being so depressed I thought several times of throwing myself in front of the buses I was taking to get from place to place,

During this time I worked two jobs in hell. One I gave up on and never forgave myself for, the other I stayed until they fired me.

Down the street from our apartments was a CVS pharmacy. This is the tale of quite possibly the worst job experience I have ever had, at least before Naziland Hamburger Hell. Again, I'll tell you more about that later on.

=+=

Now some jobs start good and go downhill from there. I was THRILLED initially with my jobs both with Cinemark and the mall. However three to four years in (especially at Cinemark having to work all day every holiday) it got old.

This job started out old.

I was not trained or given any guidelines in any way. I was told to look over a girl's shoulder at how she did the register and when she needed back up I was put on a register myself. I was not shown how to do anything so much as they waited for me to make a mistake or ask a question, when this happened they ran through the solution as fast as they could, literally too fast for me to comprehend and then snapped at me and made me feel stupid if I made the mistake again.

They went through things so fast it was clear it wasn't to SHOW me how to do anything so much as it was to shut me up so they could go back to what they were doing.

The third day in I was snapped at for forgetting my employee code number, a six digit number I needed to sign in with. I had written it down wrong and, being a little dyslexic, had transposed the first two numbers. I was screamed at and made to look like a fool in front of the other employees before I was allowed to be given my number again.

There was one female manager, I can't remember her name, I blotted it out, but she hated my guts. I was interviewed to take a management position. When I was hired I was told "Oh we're sorry, we don't have the approval to hire on and pay a manager, you're going to be a regular employee and we'll move you up." Obviously this woman thought I was gunning for her job. She was hateful to me from the start and it only got worse. She is the reason why I quit, but I'm getting head of myself.

During my first week I was given the mindless task of taking out all the "tobacco products" pipes, butane etc that was under the counter and find places for them. First I was snapped at because I hadn't had a chance to start it, stupid me, assuming that waiting on customers came first, that's what I did.

When I began the task I quickly found that NONE OF IT FIT, something she surely had to have known when she gave me the task. EVERY SINGLE ITEM was either already stocked full or there wasn't a tag or listing for it.

Then I was snapped at for doing the job too quickly. Then I was reprimanded for

for standing with my hands behind my back and told if I was ever caught on camera doing it again I would be written up. I was told to stock the cigarettes—I already had. I was then told "Well stock the candy!!", but I already had! So then I was told to clean but there was nothing to clean and in the entire four days I had worked there I had not seen any cleaning products or paper towels anywhere around. I hate jobs that are that ridiculous, where you have to make up things to do in order to not be in trouble. If your manager is not smart enough to find things for you to do, it should not be your own fault for standing around if the store is sparkling and perfectly stocked. When I tried to point this out it was then implied that I should PRETEND to clean.

I was so scared of getting caught standing with my hands behind my back, I had to pretend to stock the cigarettes—that never actually needed stocking but since I couldn't turn around and watch for customers, I got in trouble for NOT watching for customers and not greeting every one. So you were not supposed to stand idle for one single second, but if you turned around to start another task, you were snapped at because you turned your back to the customer—yet any other task you would start requires you to either turn your back to the doors or crouch down behind the counter, so you literally had to have eyes in the back of your head to do what was expected of you. It was not the single worst job I have ever had, but it was the single most ludicrous.

That night the same female manager asked me to ring her up for something that was on sale. She took out her purse and stood in front of the credit card machine (which is off to the side away from the register) so I assumed she was going to pay with a credit card. So I hit the credit card button. She snapped at me for this demanding "How did you know I was going to pay with my card?? Now I HAVE to pay with my card because you already pushed the button!!!" Actually all she would have had to do was hit cancel.

Then, in ringing up a second item, she sat the item so close to the stationary scanning gun that it rang up twice. This, again was MY fault and she blew up at me demanding to know "Why are you on a register when you don't know how to use it!?? Do I need to go back and train you again?!"

The point that I had never been trained in the first place was moot.

It also didn't seem to matter than I have been running a cash register for the last 25 years. Just because I was not trained and have not run a touch screen before, it does not mean I am incompetent.

Somewhere along the first of the second week I got in trouble for not answering the phone. Once again, no one had told me how to answer the phone, nor the company greeting, how to put someone on hold or how to transfer a call. But typically, that didn't matter, I was supposed to have learned by osmosis or something.

I worked two shifts for this manager witho being allow a break and I was so afraid of her I wasn't about to ask for one.

The turning point for me came when I was asked to do a t shirt display. The same female manager waved her arms in each direction and said (while nowhere near the actual display) one side long sleeved, one side short sleeved.

I got to the display and it was separated into four quadrants, two on each side and sure enough the shirts are jumbled. The racks were at the end of aisle 6 and 7 (one rack facing into each aisle). Now each rack had two sections, one to the inside, facing the aisle and one to the out side.

I took all the tshirts out and filled up the black column with LONG SLEEVED, arranged from small to 4x. I went on the opposite side and did the same thing.

143

Then I filled the yellow side with SHORT sleeved from small to 4x and did the same thing on the other side so that both the racks to the inner side was Long sleeved.

The female manager came out and looked at it and said 'NO! WHAT ARE YOU DOING?! ARE YOU NOT LISTENING TO ME?! I SAID (and she throws out her arms again) ONE SIDE LONG SLEEVED, ONE SIDE SHORT SLEEVED."

I said, "but I did do that, see, the side facing the interior is all long sleeved. The side facing out is all short sleeved." I said "I don't understand, do you mean Long sleeved on the left or the right?"

She said 'THERE IS NOT LEFT OR RIGHT!! JUST PUT THEM ON ONE SIDE!!'"

I asked her to show me but again she just kept waving her hands around like trying to tell a plane where to land.

So I reversed it and put all the short sleeves in the black column and all the long sleeves in the yellow column. I was sure this was it, so I called her back to look at it. This is when she exploded and asked me

"WHAT IS WRONG WITH YOU?! DO YOU NOT UNDERSTAND ENGLISH!? IF I HAD KNOWN YOU WERE ILLITERATE AND DIDN'T UNDERSTAND ANYTHING I WOULDN'T HAVE HIRED YOU! YOU'VE BEEN DOING THIS FOR THREE HOURS AND YOU STILL CAN'T DO IT RIGHT! JUST GO ON BREAK AND I'LL FIND SOMEONE WHO ACTUALLY KNOWS HOW TO TAKE DIRECTIONS!"

I asked her AGAIN, what did I do wrong. She wouldn't tell me.
It would turn out, and I had to figure this out totally on my own—that she wanted the WHOLE RACK FACING AISLE 6 SHORT SLEEVED

AND THE WHOLE RACK FACING AISLE 7 AS LONG SLEEVED regardless of the quadrants.

But she did not say this.

NEVER IN MY LIFE HAVE I EVER BEEN ACCUSED OF NOT UNDERSTANDING ENGLISH.

I have an Associates in Business with a minor in Management during which time I was Magna Cum Laude. I have a Bachelor's Degree IN English and I am CERTIFIED to TEACH English.

But that's not the point! I don't care if I just got off the plane from Siberia and all the English I knew was "Where's the bathroom?" YOU DON'T SAY THAT TO YOUR EMPLOYEE!!

That is the single most degrading, racist thing anyone has ever said to me.

I burst into tears and gave her my name tag and told her I quit. She somehow talked me into staying, I don't know how, I was so upset at the time the rest is just a blur, but I was stupid to stay.

The next day the head manager called me into his office and wanted to know why *I* was having the bad day, and told me that *his* managers would never ever say anything like that to me. Then he told me to put a smile on my face and go do my job. I did my job until the end of my shift with a smile plastered on my face and then I walked out and never came back.

CHAPTER 26

THE REDNECK ELECTRONICS STORE

I began temping on and off during that first freezing winter of starvation and unemployment. At first it was only twelve hours a week, but the jobs were actually very good and took place in nice cozy office buildings with free coffee where all I had to do was input data on spreadsheets all day. These were my salad days of near unemployment. I was trained well and treated with courtesy and respect. My hard work was appreciated and my questions were answered without me losing an appendage. However these jobs did not last.

I was offered full time temp to hire in an industrial electronics warehouse on the opposite side of town on a street that contained the dog tracks, the homeless shelters and was the main drag for hookers. It would take me an hour and a half every day to get there by bus and an hour to get home every night. However, it was work and I could not say no to it.

I asked if I needed any special skill considering I had no earthly idea what they sold. I was told no, I would just ring up sales. I'm so gullible, I'll believe anything. I had to know about things I had never heard of, I had to learn the difference between on-off-on, single pull, double throw and on(on) off, double pull double throw switches. I had to learn the difference between Cat 5 and Cat 6 cable, I had to learn what fuses went for what projects. I had to know amps and watts and pico ferrads. The first time someone said the word I thought they were saying Pico ferrets" and wondered what spicy weasels had to do with anything. I had to know the wattage of resistors, help a customer choose a transistors or help choose the right Fluke meter to measure volts, and what leads went with what meter. If you had coax cable, what cable splicers went with that, Rg6? PK5?

Needless to say I didn't understand ANY OF this shit. I was an English major whose worst subject was Math. This was Dante's inferno. The ninth circle of hell was filled with rosin core solder, RJ11 plug modulars and heat shrink tubing.

I never had much of a problem with the owners, aside from the fact that what they were trying to teach me was the equivalent of learning Chinese braille. The customers were a different matter. As you will recall at the first of this book I professed to being a Socialist/Democrat who helped elect our first black President. This did not go over well at work.

My second day on the job when I popped off to the one customer "Bush can't even speak proper English and you expected him to rebuild New Orleans??" and he looked like he was two seconds away from punching me…this told me all I needed to know about working on this side of town.

Now don't get me wrong, I respected my boss and found him to be kind, generous and extremely intelligent. He had engineering degrees, started out in aviation, first building planes, then building their communications systems, including those on Air Force One. He could answer any question anyone had whether it has to do with HAMM radios or computer circuit boards or surveillance cameras. He was a member of the yacht club and flew his own plane and sailed for fun so obviously he was no slacker and had done well for himself.

For the last week though he had been grousing about how the US is no longer a nation but a Socialist state and it's Socialist this, Socialist that and we're giving away the farm, blah blah blah.

I could sort of see his point. I guess if you're rich you think everything is gonna be taken from you and you don't want that but the rest of us are going "Hooray! We finally get a chance at the brass ring."

And I would MUCH rather listen to his point of view than the redneck oaf that looked like he was gonna take my head off. This guy said it wasn't Bush's fault that FEMA did nothing to help New Orleans because FEMA was the State's (New Orleans') responsibility to enforce. Which sort of cancels out the whole part of the FEDERAL in their name. THEN he tells me that New Orleans didn't need to be rebuilt anyway because "If '*those people*' were too stupid and poor to have insurance they deserved to lose their houses."

Oh yeah, can't have the black people recover any of their property because being poor and black means you don't deserve to have a house. Obviously. What a hillbilly backwoods retard.

After a while I'm having to hold my tongue daily. One Friday came along and it was almost time to go and right at five o'clock this guy comes in to drop off some order forms for special customer orders. He hangs around and he seemed to be flirting with me.

He asked me if I was smiling because I'm getting ready to go get drunk.

I said no actually I was getting ready to go to the tea room and have a cup of tea with my friends. He asked if I was a hippie. I just happened to have the new issue of Vanity Fair with newly elected President Obama on the cover. Just as my boss was coming out of his office I held it up and said loudly "No, I'm just a Socialist."

From the look I was given I might as well have said "I'm a Satanist."

I'm proud to have a job, I'm proud to be working class. I think everyone deserves a break. I like sharing what I have. If you already have more money than you can spend in a lifetime and someone asks you to share it, how is that a burden?

I don't think there's anything wrong with it, I think it is the way we were meant to live all along. There is such a thing as "The right thing

148

to do" only most people don't. To me, sharing, making people equal and giving the working class representation is that right thing to do.

After that day things at the KKK electronics store changed. I honestly think the other employee told the customers I was a commie because from then on it was ridiculous the looks and comments I got. There were racist jokes every day and more droppings of the "N" word than I can even count—and I can count pretty high. I held my tongue to keep my job even though I wanted to ask them what they did for bedding when all their sheets obviously had eye holes cut in them.

I stuck it out as long as I could, even though trying to learn about resistors, transistors, transformers, antenna, fuses, cat 6 cable, grounding rods and the like went FAR far beyond my realm of understanding. I learned the customers' names, even when they were rude and made me uncomfortable, I was unfailingly polite. I did everything I was told, sometimes with varying degrees of success, but I always tried my best. I hated it, I hated the people I had to deal with, I hated feeling ignorant all the time because I couldn't find the customers what they wanted or understand their problems or how to solve them.

=+=

While there, I still tried desperately to find a teaching job. Maybe they did not like the fact that I made no bones about wanting to move on quickly. However, they should have known that taking in a temporary worker with no electronics experience whatsoever, telling the temp agency it was a desk job and then performing the old switcheroo might not have made me an employee for life.

After nine months on the job, nine months of racists jokes, gay jokes, and being told that all Arabs were terrorists, despite knowing I was half Arab, I had to call in sick. I had to call in sick because at 4 am our apartment building burned down. We were awakened at three am by the smell of smoke and by the time we got out the back of the building was gone. Our unit, along with three others, did not burn but was cut into by firemen going through to the other side and suffered smoke and water damage. They cut the power to our apartment and did not let us back in to get anything. Three hundred dollars' worth of groceries in our fridge and freezer spoiled. We had no money to buy more. All the friends I thought I had, that I had been hanging out at the tea room with every night for nearly five years completely ignored me when I called them asking for help.

We had no clothes, no food and nowhere to live.

My most vivid memory of that time was sitting in a McDonalds in my pajamas with nowhere to go, nothing to do, the only things I got out of the house were my purse and our pet hermit crab and they sat on the table next to me. I opened my phone to check my email, so sure that the frantic call I had made to my friend Ylliona had been answered by all of our friends with whom I had spent the last few years hanging out with every Friday night and Wicaan holiday. The only email in my box was from Shin Solo, cussing me out because I had just confronted her about being a pathological lair. The only email in my box was from a schizophrenic girl cussing me out because I chose not to believe that she had been raped and beaten twenty times in the last two months and had ran away, lived on the street, became first a phone sex operator and then prostitute, had an abortion and still managed to graduate from the University of Memphis with full honors only to be kidnapped and raped again while at home doing her laundry.

There were no emails in my box offering help or a kind word, just Shin Solo cussing me out because, for the first time in three years. I called bullshit on one of her fantastical stories. I sat in the middle of McDonalds and began to cry, so miserable I did not care who saw me.

=+=

I called at 8 am to relate all this to my boss. "I can't come in, we have no place to live and I'm wearing my pajamas from last night." He expressed no sympathy and acted like he didn't believe me. Even though he owned two cars, two boats and a plane and could have offered assistance, he did not. When I came in the next week I was fired. I was told they found someone better and with more experience. In actuality I was pretty sure my big mouth had done me in and that they really did not believe we had suffered the loss of our apartment and maybe I was just saying this to go to yet another teaching interview.

CHAPTER 27

So, I had no job, no food, no clothes and no place to stay. As with many, many times before, once again, my sister Toni, my husband and my best buddy PJ were the only friends I had. Like we always did though, we picked ourselves up and started over. Facebook was a fairly new concept to me at the time. I posted our tragedy online in the vain hopes that all of my friends from the tea room would see it and help out. If they saw it, they didn't care, but two people I barely knew swooped in to help. Mark and Kim Dionne drove from a town forty five minutes away to help us relocate, Later, Roxann Gleason, whom I had just met and barely knew, sent us one hundred dollars to restock on food. I am overwhelmed by the kindness of strangers who became friends. I am also just as overwhelmed by the apathy of friends who turned into strangers overnight.

=+=

One month after the fire, I was offered my first teaching job. It was not in my field, it was not full time, it had no benefits and it was sixty miles away. My sister Toni helped me buy another car so I could go interview in a town I had never heard of. I went to the interview with my clothes still reeking of smoke from the fire. I was sure everyone could smell it and just as sure they would never off me the job. Happily I was wrong. I was offered and accepted a job teaching the GED program for Coastal Bend College.

My assignment was in another town, George West, still sixty miles away. My "classroom" is the dining room of the George West Chamber of Commerce.

When I accepted the job I was under the assumption there was a branch of the college IN George West and I would be teaching at that facility. When I saw the actual set up I remembered the day we had the lesson plan workshop and was told: "At some schools they will simply give you a book and say teach" which is what they did here.

I had no desk, no chalk board, no erase board, no overhead projector, no media, no access to a copier,—needless to say no computer or fax or phone…just a pile of workbooks (though not enough for everyone in the classroom, basically enough for ME and an extra set. And that's it. No heat in the winter, no air conditioning in the summer. Happy to have you, go teach.

I started out with twelve students and made the best of it, but no one wants to sit in a dark room at a card table with nothing to look at doing worksheets all day. A few stuck it out. I got three students ready to test before one went to jail and the other two just stopped coming.

They were not paying my gas and only allowing me three days a week to work. This led me to my latest stint in fast food, in which I am currently ensnared.

=+=

Teaching GED has been a tough row to hoe. I spent fifty dollars a week just on gas to get me to and from George West. George West was smaller even than my hometown. The main street had one store that housed a Radio Shack, Hallmark, Office Depot, and a drug store. I felt bad for the kids who lived there, even if they got their GED certificates, where would they work? The population sign read two thousand and the streets were almost always deserted on my drives into town.

I had no support from the judges nor the probation officers of George West. I went in to see the judge in person to plead my case, but much like Chief Wiggum in the Simpsons, the only case she ever got to the bottom of was a case of Malomars. There was a list of students, nearly twenty in all, who were under court order to attend GED classes and obtain their GED. Only one of them actually attended and the judge could have cared less. She made no phone calls and nor gave me the information to make phone calls and did absolutely nothing to even attempt to round up the kids and get them to class.

By the end of the first year I was down to two students, by the end of the first year I was fed up again. Again I set out on mission impossible and applied at every single school within a forty mile radius.

I found more work, teaching GED a little closer to home, this time only thirty minutes away but for far fewer hours. This time it was a night class which would leave my days free for regular teaching if I could be so lucky as to find it. I took it, I refused to give up on my dream of teaching.

CHAPTER 28

In the middle of teaching in George West I began to think about my mom. So many years have passed since her death that at times she does not seem real but a dream or a story I told myself once to comfort my loneliness. I have gone months without thinking of her, times that have felt like they bordered on years and then sometimes she is right there with me in my heart.

My mom had 8 or 9 brothers and 2 sisters. Out of all the kids in the family she was the only one not to graduate high school. She didn't graduate because she was pregnant with my sister Kim at 15. Now that I am much older I wonder if this had some play in my sister having so many mental problems that plagued her to the point that at 60 years of age, after countless suicide attempts, she finally killed herself.

Anyway, this was back in the fifties and I've since wondered if my mom got sent off somewhere or what. During that time, that sort of thing just did not happen.

=+=

My grandma Mimi died right before my mom (and I truly think my mom gave up her fight because Mimi was no longer around, they were so close. I think with Mimi gone she just lost the will to live) and when she did my grandfather sold the house and had it demolished. There is no piece of it left but I can still see Mimi's bedroom in my mind.

There was a huge four poster bed with blanket rail and the posters were carved and polished, but worn. The spread was lavender and the walls were off white peeling plaster. All along the top of the walls where the ceiling met the wall, around her bed, she had the graduation pictures of all my aunts and uncles and I never thought anything of it because my mom's picture was there too.

All of my uncles did not *just* finish high school, they went to college, most got degrees, two traveled the world, at least one became a doctor, one is now professor of psychology at Louisiana State. After my mom died no one on that side of the family wanted anything to do with me, I'm guessing they hated my dad or something. Either way, after my mom died I never saw any of my uncles again.

Let me get back to the photos: I remember someone talking about mom not graduating much later when I was old enough to ponder such things. I said, "But there's that picture of her on the wall, I remember it!" Someone told me then that when my mom was 20 or so she went to a photographer's studio and paid him to take a fake senior portrait of her so she could have something to hang on Mimi's wall as well.

I remembered that this week for some reason and it made me really sad. I think about that now, how she must have felt, people coming over to the house, looking at the wall and saying "Well where are you?" and her having to explain it. I think about what kind of shame she had to feel to go pay to have a fake senior picture done just to feel accepted in her own family.

My mother was not a stupid woman. One of the Wiccans I used to hang out with at the Tea Room once told me "You know how you can spot a MENSA member? When they are waiting in a restaurant, if there is nothing else to read, they will read the menu cover to cover, over and over until the food arrives."

THAT was my mom. She was never without a book in her hand. She read EVERYTHING, she painted, she wrote, she had a BRUTAL sense of humor that I clearly inherited. She had the sharpest wit and she spoke to me always like I was an adult, though I was very, very young.

I think about that with my students because I don't want any of them to ever feel left out like that, like they're not worthy of respect simply because they could not finish school in the same time frame as everyone else.

For the first time in my life I felt like my mom would be proud.

CHAPTER 29

Because of a fellow student from the alternative certification program, I found out about a job teaching Advanced Placement English at a charter school. I met with the director who pretended to love me and told me I as perfectly qualified for the job.

"However, the job does not open up until September. Would you like to sign on and substitute for us until then?"
Would I? Am I breathing?!

So I did exactly that, and believing what would be yet another lie from an educator, I quit my job in George West, believing I had a job waiting for me at home. September came and I was invited for the first teacher inservice of the year. I was so proud, I was so happy and at five pm, the day before I was supposed to start my first day I received a phone call:

"We're sorry, we sent the letter of welcome to you in error. We didn't actually hire you, it was a mistake. We sent that letter out to everyone and you're still just a substitute, so...yeah, don't show up."

It was then I realized I was stuck in Hamburger Hell.

=+=

CHAPTER 30

Working at "Burger World" (not the real name) did not start out as a bad thing. I was hired by a former customer of mine who bought nuts from me at the stand in the mall. I needed gas money, she needed an employee with experience so it seemed a fair trade. However, having been only marginally employed for several months, even after the debacle of the electronics store, I was totally unprepared for just how hard working fast food could become. I wasn't trained exactly, I never watched any videos or ran computer simulations the way all the other trainees were. They just threw me in and told me to do it.

Cashiering wasn't bad aside from the fact that the registers, while touch screen, still seemed archaic. The buttons were all odd abbreviations with no real rhyme nor reason to the set up. If anyone wanted something that did not come on the menu (add cheese, lettuce, pickles, etc or take any of these things away) you had to go to another screen, scroll through THREE MORE screens of choices. It wasn't set for breakfast separately so if you wanted to take lettuce off a burger you still had to scroll through three screens of sugar, cream, and flavor options for coffee, options for eggs: scrambled, folded, round, just to get to the burger screen. All buttons were the same color. It would have been GREAT to be able to scan and know that green meant pickles and lettuce, red meant tomatoes and ketchup, white meant mayonnaise, etc, but no!

ALL buttons were green so you had to read every single one and if your finger slipped (very easy to do on a touch screen) and you hit the wrong button you could not correct it on that screen. You had to do the entire order ALL OVER AGAIN. In a job where the amount of SECONDS you take to complete a transaction are constantly being tallied, it was the most unproductive register scheme I had ever seen in twenty years of cashiering.

This however paled in comparison to back cash. In back cash you had to navigate the incomprehensible register tabs, taking one order, while greeting, taking money from and giving the correct change back to the customer at your window. To talk to the person at the speaker box you had to press and KEEP DOWN a button on your head set, then you had to give change, while ringing up the order as it was given to you. This would actually require one set of hands to give change and one set of hands to ring up the order and hold down the button to speak to the car at the speaker. However you were expected to do all for this at once.

I was trained for this, not by a manager or even a crew trainer but by a woman whom I believe was autistic. If she wasn't, she showed all the classic signs of having Asperger's Syndrome and could not really comprehend anything outside the realm of drive through. If I asked a question she screamed at me "WHY WEREN'T YOU LISTENING WHEN I JUST TOLD YOU HOW TO DO IT??!". If I hesitated she said "Why did you apply for this job if you couldn't do it?"

I have some kind of block in my mind where I cannot listen to two things at once without panicking. If two people are speaking to me I will have to shut one out and hear the other one. If I try to hear both at once I'll have a panic attack. Drive through was clearly not for me. Luckily the assistant manager was understanding and did not try and put me back there. Until a year later. Nothing changed about my psyche, I still could not comprehend two things at once but I had no choice and learned to talk myself through the myriad of panic attacks a day in back cash would bring. I eventually had to do this because my manager at the time was such a moron, a trained monkey could have run the store better than she did. We'll get to her in a bit.

The manager who hired me quit or was fired, I'm not sure which, two months later. Then we got Tish. Tish was wonderful. I loved Tish. Tish was bi polar and rubbed a lot of people the wrong way but Tish was nothing but nice to me. However, as good of a person as Tish was, she was not much of a manger, though she was light years ahead of the idiot who came after her. Poor Tish didn't last long. She was replaced by someone I will refer to as Hamburger Hitler or just The Red Queen. She had no idea who Hitler or the Queen of Hearts were so if she reads this, which I'm sure she won't, she'll be none the wiser.

As a manager Hamburger Hitler had no earthly idea how to treat employees with respect or even a sliver of common decency. Most of the employees of this establishment had no idea that they should be treated with respect and dignity. I was educated, I knew the difference between being a manager and being a task master. I was continuously being treated like a slave from the first day McNazi turned our restaurant into her own personal Gestapo.

Several times when she first started she would interrupt me in the middle of telling her good morning to order me to get down on my hands and knees and clean something. Anyone who is so uncivil that they cannot exchange a kind greeting is not only lacking in manners but in my opinion, lacking a heart and soul. She did this her first two weeks as manager. At some point she did actually begin to say hello to her staff in the mornings however that is no excuse. If you are promoted to manager you should already know how to talk to people in a civilized manner.

=+=

In the beginning her obsession was with cleaning which blotted out any interest in customer service or food presentation. Her only objective, to which she was compulsively enthralled, is cleaning. If the customers got served in timely manner it is a coincidental side line. Many times I have been pulled off counter during "lock down" (a time when you were not supposed to leave your position) to do something idiotic like detail tables or scrub the grill area floor. Many times she started cleaning when I desperately needed back up.

160

I was reprimanded for not taking the time to wipe up spilled coffee grounds when I had a line of twenty people I was waiting on alone. Nothing she did ever made sense. She could not tell you nicely that you were doing something wrong, her tone of voice made you feel like an idiot, she spoke to you like you are a small child. It was not just me, it is not just crew members in general. She talked to her assistants like this in front of the whole staff. She didn't yell, she didn't have to raise her voice, the way she speaks to you made it clear she thought you are nothing. From the instant I met her I could not stand her and when I realized how ignorant she was I hated her that much more.

I had very limited experience in being treated like a retard but I realized in fast food you can actually get used to it.

I have two college degrees (one in business with several courses in marketing and business management), two teaching certifications, fifteen years retail management experience, and twenty five years in customer service, yet I was spoken to on a daily basis like I was five years old. When I wasn't being ordered around during her first weeks with us, I was being treated like I was her personal servant. The first three weeks she was there I spent more time cleaning than helping customers. I chose that particular place because of my background in customer service. Nowhere in my orientation was I told that every day for weeks I would be on my hands and knees detailing grout and the inside of trash bins. Had I been told I would be expected to do the job of the maintenance men as well as my own I would have passed on the employment opportunity as my knees are too worn out to do such things. She eventually toned down the non-stop cleaning, and ignoring customer service in lieu of cleaning but this hardly improved any of her management skills.

=+=

One day, she snatched a bag out of my hand and then threw the order back at me because I was not bagging it fast enough. Even if I was sixteen years old and this was my first job I would still not deserve to be treated like this. She did this to an employee who was black, and he quit. Good for him. He was one of many who did.

A week later, a black guy came in and ordered. I had the food for his order THREE TIMES and each time, before I could give it to him, she took it away from me and gave it to another customer who ordered after him. Ten customers were served before he got his order. I don't know if it was because he was black or she just didn't care whether he got his food. It was no way to treat someone who became a regular customer, though I can't fathom *why* he came back after being treated like that. This is the incident that earned her the name Hamburger Hitler—well this and the fact that every black employee we had before she took control either quit or was fired the first month of her majesty's reign.

A month later I was actually fired from the job because she said I was $25 short on my register. I was not allowed to count the register before or after my shift, nor was I allowed to watch HER count it. As a box office manager and later as concession manager at Tinseltown during the mid to late nineties I was responsible over $100,000 in petty cash that ran the box office and concession registers. I was in charge of making nightly deposits that were picked up by courier. I was never short. I have never been written up or disciplined in any way on a job for a money shortage. I can only remember one time in fifteen years that I was ever short at all. I can only assume the Red Queen expected me to go home with my tail between my legs and accept the fact that either the money had been lost or someone had intentionally taken it from my drawer because they did not want to work with me anymore. I called the home office to plead my case and twenty minutes later from the time of the phone call Hamburger Hitler called to tell me the money had somehow been "found" and asked me to come back. I did not want to come back, but I had bills to pay, so I did.

However, I did take that opportunity to stand up for myself and told her that even though she liked to treat me like I was an idiot, I wasn't and that I had twenty years in customer service and fifteen years in retail management and maybe she should keep that in mind in the future and trust that, just maybe, I do know what I am doing. Because of this, when I came back my hours were cut from 38 to 12 for the first week I was back. According to the run time/print time on the schedule I was actually taken off the schedule three hours before the money mysteriously vanished from my til and was found again.

On top of all this she went up to one of my long time customers, Herman, an elderly gentleman that comes in every day for coffee and Wi fi service, and hinted that maybe he might want to find somewhere else to hang out from now on, saying "I just wanted to let you know your little friend Joey does not work here anymore." It was not only incredibly snide and petty, but so completely unprofessional, I have no idea how this woman ever came into her management position to begin with. It certainly was not on the merit of her people skills.

I was far from the only person she harassed. The window girl, who was black, received a tip from one of her regular customers. The Red Queen demanded she hand it over, the girl refused so her majesty snatched it out of her hand and took it from her. The girl quit.

Hamburger Hitler set up interviews for prospective employees then ignored them. One day a woman came in to pick up her daughter's final pay check and she made the lady wait two hours before giving it to her. She cared about no one but herself. She wrote up one employee for calling in sick because her dad was dying of a heart attack. Another employee lost her mother in law and asked off for the funeral. She was told she had to work "at least until 6 am, that would leave you PLENTY of time to get to the funeral by 11."

I wish I was making this up. I promise you I am not.

She was a drill sergeant. She rarely asked nicely. If you have to leave at 4:00 and at 4:05 she would decide she wanted you to mop the lobby and THEN she would make a brief attempt at being nice to get what she wanted. The other 99% of the time she commanded you like you are a dog. She treated everyone the same way, like an animal.

The Red Queen, true to her name, was completely ignorant of basic human courtesy and kindness. When she wanted something from you and you did not respond fast enough, she yanked it out of your hand. When she wanted to give you something she threw it at you. It is like working with a five year old at least eighty percent of the time.

=+=

She routinely showed up to work hours late. When she would show up, she would either be on her cell phone, hiding in the office or sitting in the lobby in the middle of the breakfast rush, leaving me to run window with no back up alone. The only "help" she offered was to complain that I wasn't doing enough to move drive through and I had forgotten to wipe a customer's cup down. Had I not been stocking, cooking hash browns, brewing coffee, bagging orders, putting orders in the correct order to hand out, greeting customers, getting drinks, condiments, refills and handing out orders at the window alone maybe the drink cup would have been clean.

As soon as she seized power three fourths of our employees either quit or were fired. Not only did the regular employees leave in droves, but assistant managers as well. Under her reign our restaurant became a revolving door where some people only worked one day before calling it quits. They left because of the way she treated people.

She hired people so ignorant they thought it was okay to give elderly customers regular coffee if they ordered decaf and just tell them it was decaf because they were too lazy to brew another pot. When I explained to her the health hazards of doing this, she gave me a blank stare and asked "How do you know this?!" like I had just tried to explain the theory of time travel. She hired employees so ignorant they could not tell burger patties from chicken. I am not kidding. She hired these people because she wanted to be surrounded by her peers.

An employee, who of course promptly quit asked to be let off early to rehearse for her roles in "A Mid-Summer Night's Dream." Hamburger Hitler made a face and said "Is that a movie? I never heard of it." I wish I was making that up, I am not. When we had a water line break for three hours leaving us without any of our beverage stations, she refused to take the call from our assistant manager and slept in. Later she yelled at the manager for poor sales as he tried to explain to her we had nothing to serve the customers: no coffee, no juice, no cappuccino, no tea, no sodas. She thought a water line break meant we just couldn't serve sodas but the same line goes to every single drink station. She ran her own store and yet was completely ignorant as to how things worked.

=+=

I began to learn to work without having a break. No one was allowed a break no matter how much they worked. Ten hours, eleven hours straight, hot, miserable and dehydrated, this was the constant state of affairs once Tish, our former manager, was replaced. I began compiling incident days and times in order to make a formal complaint to our supervisor who was over our store and four others. The letter was completely ignored but in researching Texas labor laws I came to sadly realize that employees are not guaranteed get breaks and there is no legal recourse for me in this matter. And people wonder why I'm a Socialist.

Do you have ANY idea how hard it is to glue a smile on your face and present a happy front to customers when it is ninety five degrees both inside and out, you have not eaten all day, you haven't had anything to drink, you have been working and moving non stop for eight hours and if you slag or slow down even in the slightest you're nagged at hatefully for losing seconds in counter or drive through times? It is *very* hard to treat your customers like royalty when you yourself are being treated like an animal. A split second after you are being snapped at for not being fast enough and you are sick and exhausted and thirsty and on the verge of tears from being snapped at and ordered around all day long, you have to put a smile on your face and act like the happiest person in the world so your customers don't know what's going on. It is a hard thing to do on a daily basis.

Her management skills were as horrible as her people skills. We were constantly out of everything from salt to coffee to buns. One weekend we served all the customers decaf and told them it was regular because she forgot to order coffee. And for all her bluster and frenzy of cleaning, once she settled in we NEVER had enough sanitizer, floor cleaner, dish soap or laundry detergent for our towels. Have you ever seen the movie Zombieland? The part where Columbus says one of the things he's scared of is the cleaning rags they use to wipe down tables in chain restaurants? I'm here to tell you he had every right to be afraid. A lot of the time the ONLY reason we had cleaning supplies was because I brought them from home. This was usually a moot point because the people she hired were completely ignorant of the such basic concepts of cleaning as the concept of the three compartment sink. I watched in horror one day as a girl she wanted to promote to crew leader poured a filthy bucket of mop water into a sink of clean, sanitized dishes and gave me a deer in the headlights look when I screamed "What are you doing?!" This girl is still the primary cook. She wears a pin that says "Don't make me poison your food" and I rarely eat on my break if she is the one preparing it. This wasn't as good of a story as the overweight hood rat who worked there when I first started. Each day she would take one of the large stickers that said "USE FIRST" and slap it on her ass and prance around with it on there for the rest of her shift, waiting for customers to comment on it. I actually think she went on to manage another store.

Getting back to poor management and the inability to count product or order anything we actually needed, we would have pancakes but no syrup, coffee, but no sugar or cream. We had sugar and cream but no stir sticks. We would open hours late because the manager who was scheduled would oversleep or just wouldn't show up at all. Nothing ever happened to these managers and no one seemed to care about all the business we lost on these occasions. Sometimes I think the customers showed up just for the entertainment of the train wreck which has become the day to day workings of our store.

We were always short on product. Either it was missing insane amounts of something, like missing 50,000 chicken nugget, or other things that no one in their right mind would steal, like three whole cases of cup lids. We came to the conclusion early that The Red Queen simply couldn't count. This was illustrated not only in missing product but in schedule making where the bulk of employees would get off at one time, say 2pm, but no one else would be scheduled until 5. This left the entire store with no staff for three hours causing all staff involved in the morning shift to stay late. This happened almost every day.

Her short sightedness knew no bounds. When we first began to be short on product, rather than entertaining the notion that she could be wrong with her counting, she became convinced that someone was intentionally throwing away food. What was her intelligent solution for this? She threw away all our trashcans so we had nothing to toss our trash in. We had special trashcans made especially to fit in between the grills and these were tossed in the Dumpster, all the other trash receptacles were thrown out as well. She was shocked when this did not solve the problem and only caused the store to look more trashy. No food meant nothing to serve the customer. Between not having product, having faulty equipment and assistant managers who had no earthly idea how to manage, every day was like entering a three ring circus of failure.

A typical day would go like this, someone would order a sausage sandwich and whoever opened would forget to start the sausage on time. Have you ever seen the Wedding Singer when Adam Sandler tells his ex-fiancé "Once again, things that could've been brought to my attention YESTERDAY!"? There was a lot of that going on at work.

I would come in at six am go to back cash and start taking orders, a customer would order a biscuit and AFTER I would ring it up someone would come running in from the back to inform me the oven was not working. Or the managers would listen via the head sets to make sure I was offering pies to every single customer as was something we had to do with each sale. They would listen, not say a word until a customer actually ordered on and then tell me "Oh we don't have any..." SOMETHING I COULD HAVE BEEN INFORMED OF WHEN I FIRST WALKED IN THE DOOR. This left ME to look like an ass and having to apologize to the customers for offering them something we didn't even fucking sell.

The Red Queen never took heed of upcoming promotions or special pricing. The customers would come in asking about some new food item they had seen advertised on tv and since The Red Queen had absolutely no foresight in researching anything other than the fastest route through the buffet line at Golden Corral, we could not answer any of the customers' questions.

One morning in drive through a woman yelled at me, after a full week of us not having sugar for her coffee, "Do you have any idea how fucked up your store is?! It is totally, completely fucked up!!"

All I could say was "Yes Ma'am, I agree with you. Our store is completely fucked up and for that I apologize." I turned around and Hamburger Hitler was right behind me. She said nothing and walked away. If she was upset by this comment, she certainly did nothing to ever correct the problem.

On the crew survey when asked to comment on management I said this "I imagine that she was raised in a barn by animals because this is how she treats people." I went on to compare her management style to that a famously vile German dictator. I did this because I thought maybe the supervisor or franchise owner would read it and want to know why I compared their manager they had hired, they had trained and they had promoted to Adolf Hitler. They didn't care. I brought up the myriad of short comings of The Red Queen to her supervisor time and time and time again. Each time the female supervisor just made excuses and told me I needed to be patient while the idiot developed her skills. After a while I had to assume the only reason nothing was done was that the two of them were having an illicit lesbian affair. Now before you get all hot and bothered at me saying this, let me assure you it would be like sexual congress between two sea cows.

I wish I could point to one thing and say "This was the pinnacle of retardation that I dealt with on this job." However, unfortunately, as I write this I am still employed there and every day is more mind numbingly revolting than the last. I knew all hope was lost of finding any common ground when my boss—Hamburger Hitler, Queen Hitler, The Red Queen, She Who Shall Not Be Named, Nazi Bitch Barbie— hit me up in the stockroom for drugs. ME…who tells anyone who'll listen "I'm straightedge so I don't do shit.". Me, the woman who has worn three Xs on her belt every day for a year. Me, the girl with three Xs tattooed across my now untoned middle aged stomach. I guess Hamburger Hitler thought this made me a porn star because she elbowed me in the stock room and asked if I was holding on Lortab. I wasn't. She however was holding…THE TITLE OF THE STUPIDEST PERSON I HAVE EVER HAD THE DISPLEASURE OF WORKING FOR.

CHAPTER 31

When I started out I didn't think being a teacher was an unobtainable dream. It was not like being a rock star or an athlete or a singer or dancer. I scored high on my tests, I did well in class, I loved teaching kids. I thought this was enough. I might as well have quite my job at the mall to play scratch off lotto tickets every day for three years. Who knew that wanting to be a teacher was about as realistic as wanting to date Katy Perry? I live in a town where every single girl gets pregnant before they are seventeen and drops out of school, populating the lower grades with kids of their own over and over and over again. I thought this meant job security. What it actually meant was that no one wants to hire or work with anyone as smart, or smarter than they are. Not only is ignorance bliss, in Corpus Christi, ignorance is cherished, sacred way of life.

I have gone through periods of extreme depression after leaving the mall job, so sure I would get a teaching job right away only to be denied at every turn.

I had all these friends, the Wicaans, the Tango Tea Room crowd that believe in 'giving back to the universe' and karma and all that and I really truly used to believe in it as well.

But I had been 'giving back to the universe' my whole life. When I began my instruction with the alternative certification program I stopped cutting my hair. Initially it was for good luck but as luck would have it not having a job would mean no money for haircuts…or facials, or massages or manicures or anything else I had gotten used to while working at the mall. I decided later on that when I got my first teaching job, no matter what it was, I would cut my hair off and give it all to Locks of Love as a thank you to the universe. Upon getting the job in George West I did exactly that, cutting thirteen inches off my hair. If the universe was pleased it made no sign of it to me.

The universe totaled two cars back to back when OTHER people ran red lights, turned around and sued US and our insurance wouldn't back us.

The universe saw fit to give jobs that I studied ten years to be qualified for to high school drop outs with no experience. When I left my job in the mall I lost my insurance and after a while we had no more money for the gym and no transportation to get there even if we'd had the funds. I gained back all the weight I had lost when I first became edge and suffered terrible pain with each monthly cycle that finally got chalked up to "hormones" which was the community clinic's way of saying "We don't know and you're not paying anyway so fuck off." So the universe saw fit to let me experience being a skinny bitch for a few years and then took it all way.

The universe lured me away from the job I had with promises of a better job that I was much more suited for that I would actually enjoy, only for me to find out that in today's economy there was no way on earth I could actually achieve that job(teaching). The universe left me to work in Hamburger Hell with a manager half my age, with one fourth of my education and a tenth of my intelligence. F U Universe!

There were times I felt positive I had wasted my entire life being a good, honest, intelligent, hard working person for absolutely nothing. At one point I was sure If I'd had any inkling this was the way the world worked, I would have started popping out kids at 13 like everyone else in the state. Hell, if I'd gotten on welfare then I would have been set for life—dumb and fat but set for life.

However this was not the way I was raised and though I continue to struggle I do so completely on my own without government assistance. Everything happens for a reason and things that are meant to be come to pass so there must be some divine reason why I am stuck in Hamburger Hell.

There was a reason I did not kill myself when I was thirteen or eighteen or twenty five.

There was a reason why I lost all the friends I thought I had and all the girls I loved so much and tried to mentor ended up hating me.

CHAPTER 32

I don't remember when I joined facebook or why and I do not remember how I came upon the profile of my friend Kim Acrylic. I just remember seeing a photo of a very hot punk girl with cotton candy pink hair and being smitten, but fearing she was probably under age and thinking I probably should keep my mouth shut about it. I thought Kim was under age and because of me having the name I do, Kim thought I was a man. We were both wrong and once we started talking we became friends. Kim kept telling me about being a published author and at first I was so jealous thinking how someone so young had gotten published before me. Then I realized she was actually of age and I ordered her book. That was the beginning of me believing I could be published too.

I took all the pain, anger and depression of the last several years, I took my trials and triumphs of being straightedge and my journey and turned them into my first book of poetry. It was an amazing experience. It gave me a chance to talk to the first straightedge guy I ever knew, Chris, getting his blessing to use his name. Talk was all I did, though my husband still swears we are having some big clandestine straightedge affair (if there is such a thing). He wrote me about six lines on myspace and told me he hoped the book made me a millionaire. For a Socialist to tell you he hopes you make money beyond your wildest dreams, it can only be taken as an insult. He may as well have said "fuck you", but again, at least he was honest, which is more than I can say for most of the people I know. I'm sure he never bought a copy but I would like to think his ego made him just to see himself mentioned.

I gave copies to Hayat and Zeke who glowed with pride as if I were their real daughter. It was a big deal, they took me out to eat at the mall, which on a pensioners fixed income was a big deal. I bought books for each of them and wrapped them, each had a different autograph in it, specific to each one of them. They then took me around to meet some of their other Middle Eastern friends who ran shops at the mall and showed them my book, again as if they were my real parents. Hayat was true to her nature though and demanded "Did you put that dancing girl on the cover?!" I said no, it was the call of the publisher. "You see, that is all Middle Eastern women are in the US, Burka wearing belly dancers! And look at what they did to your name!! Your Arab name is half the size on the cover as your Arab name. Look! LUKE in big letters and Jabor in small! What does that tell you?!" God love her, she was right on all counts, but I still knew she was proud of me.

I called my sister Toni in the Virgin Islands and I could hear the excitement in her voice. She asked my permission to announce it in our hometown newspaper. She also bought extra copies and we debated on which family members could handle my poems about making out with other girls. I was a bit distraught at this because I had really not taken into account anyone from the far ends of the family tree reading my work. PJ assured me that Dad would be so proud of me. I said "No he wouldn't, not after he read I liked girls, he'd disown me. " PJ replied "Oh Joey, you know we'd have given your dad the EDITED version!!" I loved her for that.

I got to share my story with many people and more than that, through my poetry I got to keep Margo alive and share her life and spirit with those who never knew her so her memory lives on. It was good for me too, after years of dealing with issues of abandonment and being so hurt and so depressed that I could not save all those I loved, save them from the world, save them from themselves. Through writing that book I forgave them, I forgave myself and I got closure.

I was also able to give a parting gift to the owners of the Tango Tea Room, the place I used to think of as my second home. I would go there every Friday night for years. At first it was just me and Ylliona and then this whole little community sprang up around her and I was just a hanger on, along for the ride. I met MENSA members, computer programmers, lawyers, geologists, teachers, hippies, stoners, nurses, Indians, witches, warlocks, Wicaan priests and more free spirits than you can shake a didgeridoo at. Under the stars in the courtyard, listening to drum circles play and resonate into the night or sitting inside the fabric draped walls I spent the best Friday nights of my life dining on hummus, drinking herbal tea and chai lattes and having the most intelligent, intriguing, fun and interesting conversations known to man. Of all these people, after the fire, Frank Kelly is the only one to still talk to me. God bless him. He's still trying to convert me to Republicanism. Asking a Socialist to become a Republican is like asking a straightedger if you can buy him a beer. It's not happening. But I love him for not giving up on me like everyone else did and encouraging me and my writing and my pursuit of education.

I took The girl who loved Jade Puget and The generic scene girl from Austin to the tea room, I took my friend John Fanning and my husband to the tea room. The tea room was my sanctuary until like Eve biting from the apple of knowledge, I dared to ask why no one ever came to our aid when we had our fire. I was never invited out again.

So one day, a year after the fire, I got this email through the Tango Tea Room email list saying the owners were giving up the Tea Room and going to travel the world. They had already been commissioned to do documentaries for the Travel Channel so I knew it was pretty much only a matter of time before they left this piece of shit city. I wrapped up my book to give to them as a going away present and took off downtown, not knowing if anyone would even be there or not. The crazy thing was, as soon as I walked in the door they knew who I was! I couldn't believe they remembered me. But I guess seeing me around every weekend for 8 years rubbed off even if I was too shy to say anything. I gave them a copy of my book to say thank you and to remember Corpus by.

They were so nice and seemed so excited and hugged me tight and told me thank you. Around us the tea room was being dismantled, all the wonderful things, the incense, scented oils, jewelry, handmade clothing and scarves and bags were being boxed up.

At any other time it would have seemed very sad. The best nights of my life were spent in that place and most of the poems in that book were composed there. Three or four even mention the place. But instead I left feeling warm and loved and excited for their coming adventures off into the world.

And to think this all began because I saw a picture of a girl with cotton candy pink hair and wondered if I should hit on her or not. I'm giving my hormones a high five. After causing me to go from a size 5 to a size 14, it's the least they could do to pay me back.

=+=

As I write this I am still working in Burgerland Hell and waiting on my big break to be a full time teacher. There are rumors afoot, rumors that Hamburger Hitler knows her fate has been sealed by dozens of crappy grading by supervisors and surprise visits by corporate big wigs. Supposedly she is transferring to another hamburger franchise down the street. We are all waiting with baited breath. I'm not sure it will ever happen. I have learned in the fast food business, in particular the company I work for, retardation is rewarded, hard work is punished, and the logical will never win out. We may be stuck with Hamburger Hitler for life, stuck with doing dishes with Sun Laundry detergent and promoting managers that scream at employees and call them names in front of customers. If The Red Queen is ousted, wonderful. If not, I will not be surprised. I feel like this is Fast Food Survivor: Out Play, Out Wit, Out Last.

However, right before submitting this to the publisher, I awoke to the headline that our Republican governor, Gov. GoodHair is cutting the education funding of our state by EIGHT BILLION DOLLARS. BILLION. Insane ideas are being batted around like doing away with first, second and twelfth grade and only sending children to school from third until eleventh. As if it is not bad enough that seventy five percent of the girls in this town get pregnant at fifteen and schools are overburdened and underfunded, teachers are outnumbered, threatened and beaten up by students, now we are going to have what little funding is there taken from us. Waking up to these headlines may just mean I have as much of a chance of getting a teaching job as I do of winning the lottery. However I do continue to dream.

What have I learned?

I think I have learned to live in the moment. I reference this not from the catch phrase of wrestlers Matt and Jeff Hardy who used the expression to excuse a life spent doing drugs and acting like morons, but Eckhart Tolle. I have learned to try and make the best of the situation I am in and to look forward and do my very best not to look back, though not looking back is a full time job itself.

The job at Burger World has not been totally horrible. It has its own cast of characters just like the mall did and I have learned to enjoy simple things like the variety of customers I wait on. There is the old lady who owns two Mercedes cars and comes in every day just to pay half price for a senior coffee. She is very kind and always asks about me when I am not there. There are the cute geeky Asians that come in, ruining thousands of years of good, simple, low fat eating habits by patronizing our restaurant. They order fish sandwiches with orange juice or spicy chicken with mushroom or anything with iced coffee no matter the time of day or night. One particular group came in every week day for an entire semester. The guys in this group were especially cute and so I decided I was going to impress them. I learned some phrases in Japanese, practiced for two weeks and then tried it out on them. It turned out they were Chinese and I had totally offended them. They were not impressed.

There were the look alikes too. The Kyle McLauclan look alike drove a Mitsubishi and had toured China and yet came in twice a week to patronize the dollar menu and take advantage of the free wi-fi. Two guys who worked as painters and looked exactly like Kenny Chesney and Travis Barker came in every day for lunch. There was a guy who looked just like Tim Robbins who would come in for decaf, but sadly, the guy who looked exactly like Jeff Daniels had no idea who Jeff Daniels was.

There were guys that didn't exactly look like anyone in particular but were still good looking. Two regular lookers were Andy, the metrosexual undertaker. Yes, you read that right. Andy looked like what would happen if Jade Puget of AFI ever had to shave his sideburns and get a real job. If I died in Corpus I would have no problem with Andy being the one to drain my blood...if he even did that. I actually have no idea what his true vocation was other than he worked at a local funeral home. The other man was known only as "The sweet tea guy" because he came in almost every day and that was all he ordered. He was extremely good looking in the generic businessman sort of way that I normally would have never found attractive. However I would literally push people out of the way to be the one to get his iced tea. Yeah, I'm a dork.

Then there was Buddy Holly. I guess you could call Buddy Holly my burger crush. True to the Elvis Costello archetype that I always seemed to fall for, he was tall, had short dark hair, geeky glasses, and actually looked more like Rivers Cuomo. The first time he walked in and ordered, he was wearing a Weezer t shirt. For the next week all I could hear in my head was the song "Buddy Holly". The next time he came in I asked "Hey, you had a Weezer shirt on last time didn't you?" He was surprised i remembered and I told him how, because of him, I couldn't stop singing Buddy Holly. From then on when he came in I called him Buddy Holly and, like most of my regular customers, I had memorized his order.

I read somewhere once that the person you are destined to be attracted to is ingrained in you before you reach age five. I'm not sure who hypothesized this but it always struck me as odd. The only way this would have been true of me was if I had somehow stumbled on a Superman comic as a toddler and fallen for Clark Kent. The dark hair, those geeky glasses…they stop my heart every time. I will surely have a geek fetish until the day I die and I have no idea why.

Do you remember the movie The Water Boy with Adam Sandler? One day I never forgot at Burgerland was meeting the real life Farmer Fran, the coach with the pierced nipples that no one could understand. While working counter a whole family from Louisiana came in. I knew where they were from because they were all decked out in LSU gear and had the requisite accents. They all had multiple facial piercings… all of them, mom and dad and all three teenagers. Being the smart ass that I am, I had to ask "Was there a two for one special at the piercing parlor?". To this the father replied "Well darlin', let me show you!" He pulled up his shirt and showed me his pierced nipples, right in front of his kids and wife. I should have had hysterical blindness at that moment but God was not that kind.

I also made a great friend named Madalyn. She is the only real friend I made there, though two of the managers not only were competent but were compassionate, intelligent and just very cool all-around individuals. How THEY survived so long in Burgerland I will never know. The crazy thing about Maddie is that she looks, acts and sounds EXACTLY like my old friend Grendel. Crazy, huh? Everything comes full circle. Maybe you just have to live long enough to get around to it again.

Much like the mall, not all the people I saw were ones I wanted to fraternize with. There was one guy who came through the drive through about once every few months to get an iced coffee. He looked EXACTLY like Charles Manson. Another regular customer was a creepy old man. Every single time he came in he had very young teenage boys in tow, all of them wearing as little as the weather permitted. They were all good looking kids and they all looked utterly distressed and terribly uncomfortable. They never met my gaze. He would always make a big deal about how he was buying them all lunch. It was never the same set of boys twice but they all shared the same scared look, like they were ten seconds from running out the door. It probably sounds innocuous, but it was absolutely creepy. Everyone else noticed too. Finally one day I decided I was going to put him on the spot to see what he'd say. When he got in my line I said "How come I always see you buying lunch for pretty boys and yet I never see you with any pretty girls." He looked at me and replied "Well they live with me and I help them out. Besides, girls are dangerous. I much prefer boys."

Ew.

As simple as it was, this was my entertainment. It kept me from sticking my head in the fryer when I was surrounded by people half my age with a fourth of my education and a tenth of my intelligence. At first I resented or looked down on them, and finally I learned to accept that this was where I had been place, by God, the Universe and everything. I made my peace with it, trying to find the entertainment value in it all. At forty I expected to either be writing for the Austin American Statesman or settling into a role of English professor at a nice liberal college. Instead, I was serving burgers and fries alongside people who dropped out of school in the eighth grade. Maybe it is my punishment for being such an elitist bitch, maybe it is a lesson in finding the good in all things, no matter how soul crushing and spirit breaking they may appear to be.

I have learned that honesty is more precious than gold. It is in rare supply and should be cherished. And I don't mean the type of honesty where you finally tell someone you hate to go fuck themselves. That kind of honesty is just hate in disguise. I'm talking about telling someone the truth, the no frills, non dressed up honest truth, whether it be "I'm not edge any more and I wanted you to hear it from me" or "Why were you so obsessed with me? I always thought I was kind of a jerk!" or anything that comes from the heart and is not meant to be deliberately unkind.

I have learned that whoever said "Time heals all wounds" is not the fucking moron I thought he was. However, time is relative. If you expect the hurt to go away in a month, or six or twelve, you are just naive. It can take years, it can take decades and it never truly goes away but you learn to love that hurt because it is part of you it is who you are. You nurture it and soothe it and polish it until the rough edges are gone and it is smooth and malleable and slips back into your heart with hardly any pain at all, just the weight of it remains.

There are some people I will never forgive, like my step mother and the addict who killed my best friend. Everything else turns to beads of water sliding from the shiny green iridescent feathers of a duck's back. It slides down into all that water under the bridge and flows away. All those who left me I still love. My family, my friends, the girls I thought of as my daughters, most of which I have distanced myself from for my own mental health. Still, I love them deeply and always will.

Did you ever see the Xmen movie? When Rogue tells Wolverine that after she stole his power to heal herself she still feels his presence in her blood? It is like that with every person I have ever loved, tried to help, lost, mourned for, watched walk away or die. You are all still inside me. We did the best we could, we failed, life went on. If I never told you I loved you, I am telling you now. If you thought I took it back, I didn't.

Out of everything, I have learned that love is the most important thing of all and as cliché as it sounds, it does start with loving yourself. If you have the love of someone else, then you are lucky indeed.

A GROOVY KIND OF LOVE

I have learned that my husband is my best friend. We will never see eye to eye on the subject of controlled substances but he has stood by me without fail. He put a Tazzmission lock on kid who was hitting on me at the mall and the kid nearly passed out. Needless to say the kid never hit on me again. He has gone after people who hurt me. We are two sides of the same coin. We laugh at the same jokes, quote the same movie lines and turn and stare at the same hot women. To this day he is still jealous of sXe Chris who never even gave me the time of day, and that, in its own way is endearing. We make jokes and speak in a language of song lyrics, movie lines, wrestling catch phrases and SNL skits that no one else would understand.

The times I'm sure he won't understand me are the very times he comes through. One weekend The girl who called herself Mikey Way, one of the very emotionally messed up girls I tried to help, faked her own suicide online. She wrote me a suicide note and dropped off the radar for three days. Before this she would go mental if I did not spend anything less than six hours every night chatting with her online. I was sure she was dead and in hysterics. I had a seventy two hour panic attack for which my husband was ready to take me to the ER and force tranquilizers down my throat, which I wouldn't allow because of my edge. I sobbed nonstop all weekend and ended up in a state of absolute physical and mental exhaustion. I was fully expected him to say "This is what you get for trying to help people." Finally she logged on and claimed she'd tried to OD and it didn't work. I have no idea if this is true because after six years of trying to help her she told me everything she had ever told me about her life was a lie, then blocked me from her email and reported *me* as stalking *her.*

Anyway, I sat in front of the computer, taking my first real breath in days when he came into the room and I explained what was going on. Tears streaming down my face I said "You know, maybe I should have just had kids. Maybe if I would have had one of my own, none of this shit would have ever happened." He put his arms around me, wiped my face and said "You know that's not true. You know that even if you'd had kids of your own, you'd still have spent your life trying to save the lives of everyone else. That's why I love you."

He is the only guy in the world I would have had a conversation like this with:

A Typical Conversation Between Hubby and Me, Proving We are just NOT your Average Couple
{Pink comes on the radio}
A: Oh look at that, it's the girl Tim Armstrong called the greatest female singer of our time! ha (laughs sarcastically)

J: Pfffffffffffffftt! The best female singer he boned this week maybe!

A: You know if she was going to go after some old rocker dude, she could have done so much better. I mean, really.

J: Yeah, I *guess*. Like Rollins or Mike Ness.

A: What do you mean you GUESS? Armstrong is an ugly bastard!

J: No he's not!! I'd still do him!! He's still good looking!

A: *You'd fuck Tim Armstrong*?! I mean, I know you'd give Glenn Danzig a mercy fuck and all….
J: Yeah, if old man Danzig could get it up I'd certainly give it to him!

A: But Tim Armstrong?!

J: You're damn right I would!! But…he'd have to keep the bandanna on. I mean, I couldn't take the no teeth thing and the no hair thing all at once! I'd just have to keep my eyes shut and keep thinking
"The hot tattoos, think of the hot tattoos!" Plus, you know he's probably done Davey. That's a turn on right there.

A: Oh god. Ew. Well if you get to fuck Tim Armstrong, then I get to fuck Brody.

J: You can HAVE Brody's skanky ass! Just make sure you wear a condom!

A: ME?! You make Armstrong wear a condom! He's got more diseases than she does!

J: Doubtful.

A: Meow! Aren't we catty!?

J: I'd share Pink with ya, but you'd have to let me do Carey Hart too.

A: You think Carey Hart is hot?

J: Yeah, but just cuz of his ink.

A: Okay, you can bone Carey Hart but if you do that, you give up the right to share Lita with me.

J: Noooooooooooooooooo!! I wanna do Lita too!!! If I give up Carey Hart can I fuck Jeff Hardy?

A: Yes but only because Jeff Hardy is so gay, he's technically a woman!
J: YAY!!!!

=+=

I feel my life has become full circle. I have rediscovered and reconnected with friends like Kathy Dean, Amy Williamson, Lisa French and Christy Boland who knew me as a child, loved me then, before I was straightedge or cool, or an elitist bitch out to save the world, And they love me still today. I feel so, so lucky to have them back in my life.

I am not cool, I am not hip, I am not hardcore and I cannot change the world. Just your average straightedge, middle age , music obsessed, ultra-literate, punk rock, semi employed English teacher. I couldn't save the world, I could barely save myself, but you know what? I regret nothing. I put myself out there and loved and laughed and tried my best. I was hurt, I was abandoned, I was led astray and lied to but I am still here, still proud, still true to myself.

EPILOGUE: LOVE AS A MIX TAPE AND OTHER ASIDES

With great apologies to Rob Sheffield here are my mixes, some poetry and a few other endings.

Mix for The girl who called herself Mikey Way

Beautiful—Ten Years
Last Tattoo—Rehab
Betrayed—Avenged Sevenfold
Stars All Seem To Weep—Beth Orton
Dead—My Chemical Romance
Cold Hands—AFI
Endlessly She Said—AFI
In the End—Linkin Park
Straight Outta Line—Godsmack
Subway Funeral—Thursday
Inside The Fire—Disturbed
You Were The Cancer—Thursday
Trashed and Scattered—Avenged Sevenfold
Liar—Rollins Band

Mix for The girl who loved Jade Puget and The generic scene girl from Austin

Desecrate Through Reverence—Avenged Sevenfold
One Wing—Wilco
Savior—Rise Against
Pretty Girls—Neko Case
Ashes of American Flags—Thursday
Miss Murder—AFI

Somebody That I Used To Know—Elliot Smith
My Life Inside Your Heart—Rise Against
Ready to Fall—Rise Against
All My Life—Foo Fighters
Teenagers—My Chemical Romance
Blood to Bleed—Rise Against
Times Like These—Foo Fighters
Holocaust—Placebo
Six Ways Til Sunday—Rise Against

The Female of the Species…
Recollections of those who have come and gone in my life

Joey and her sidekick

Joey D I met in the sixth grade because she was the only girl in town with the same first name as me. Only girl I knew for probably 20 years that had the same first name as me.

She always wore the best clothes the 80's had to offer. Little did I know that her mom was pulling 12 hour shifts at a bank to buy her those clothes. Her mom and dad divorced when she was six so her mom overcompensated by giving her everything she ever wanted.

Joey had a best friend, a sidekick. In high school, her sidekick was just a snobby bitch. She had a lot of money and she made sure everyone knew it. We had nothing in common. We somehow all met because we all listened to Duran Duran.

Joey also hung out with a girl named Claudia. Claudia moved when we were sophomores. The one thing I remembered about Claudia is that she wore her hair in French braids with metal snap barrettes that were color coordinated with whatever outfit she was wearing. Joey, her sidekick and Claudia were a clique. I insinuated myself in with them because they were the only girls I knew my age that listened to Duran Duran like I did. They didn't seem to like me but I didn't care.

After Claudia moved she and Joey lost touch but before, she, Joey and her sidekick were all best friends. I had a couple of friends myself but for some ungodly reason I REALLY wanted to be in their clique.

Well with Claudia gone, Joey and her sidekick sort of adopted me into their circle. It was grudging at first but then her sidekick helped me with a job at the movie theater and Joey and I stayed friends after high school. Once we were college aged and older we did EVERYTHING together for years.

I was always the poor best friend. Joey and Her sidekick were always paying for me. For Joey it was no big deal but her sidekick made a huge show of it. She helped me with my job, helped me to advance, and her family sort of just adopted me into their own. When I moved to Corpus it was because her sidekick put in a good word for me with the general manager of the sixteen screen theater there. Her sidekick went first and I followed. For a while her sidekick and I lived in Corpus and Joey still lived back home. With me being in the same town her sidekick and I seemed to get very close.

Well, Joey met a really hot guy and they got married. Right before the wedding she finds Claudia Gonzales again. It turns out everyone was living in Dallas right next to each other and they never knew it.

I went to Joey's wedding(this was when I was a size 4), was reunited with everyone and had a blast. It was a dream of a night, we were all together, all of us, friends from high school. The only one missing was Margo. As we danced to Duran Duran for hours on end at the reception and drove through Dallas at night in the limo singing "Young Americans" by David Bowie at the top of our lungs, it was like the last fifteen years had not even happened and we were still 16 again. I kept waiting for Joey's mom to yell "Turn that shit down!" but it didn't happen. Time had passed, we had grown up.

It was the last memory of them I have and I'm glad it's a good one. As soon as Claudia was back in the picture her sidekick stopped talking to me and wanted nothing to do with me. Joey speaks to me once in a blue moon, but it's not like we're still best friends. The only thing we talk about now is the television shows we watch. I know nothing of her life, she doesn't share. Through a few online interactions I have learned that I'm not being paranoid, Claudia and her sidekick really do hate my guts. They did well at pretending for Joey's sake at the wedding weekend, I'll give them that.

Her sidekick, having never been married, and actually never had a steady boyfriend by age 30, decided she knew relationships far better than I. When my husband started drinking she absolutely demanded that I leave him. When I didn't take her advice at the moment she gave it, she pretty much told me any abuse I suffered was deserved and made me feel like shit. When I separated from my husband in my own time and with no one's help I went back to her, somehow thinking she'd be pleased with me. She refused to talk to me.

Years later when I quit my job at the mall, I started having to track down recommendations for jobs. The theater had been sold to another company and the man who hired me on was long gone but I had worked with Her sidekick for 7 years. I never missed a day of work with her and she knew how much of a hard worker I was. She saw that I worked my way up from concession girl to assistant manager of a sixteen screen theater. I asked if I could use her as a reference because she was my only link to my theater job. She flat out refused. That was the last time I spoke to her.

So basically for 20 years I was a replacement friend until the other chick, Claudia, came back. I wasn't a real friend, not worth the time once my replacement was found, I was a stand in. I was an extra in my own life.

I still dream about Joey and her sidekick at night. In most of the dreams they are angry with me, leaving me behind somewhere. In about ten percent we are still friends and my world is perfect.

Ylliona: From Germany with ~~love~~

I met Ylliona through an ad I placed on AOL. She placed a similar ad and we met. The only difference between our ads being that she placed hers because she was new in town and wanted to meet people; I placed my ad because I was looking for a date. She never figured that out and I never had the heart to tell her. Like with anything else in my life, my luck with girls was pretty laughable. When it comes to girls I am still a 40 year old virgin and have long since given up on any such romantic pursuits, which I must add were a hundred percent endorsed by my husband.

We had little in common except that we were both very intelligent and tended to look down on others who weren't. Despite this we quickly became very good friends. We did so many fun things together, went on so many adventures and shared so many inside jokes, I could not in good conscience kill enough trees to write them down on. It started with just me and Ylliona. Ylliona was the big bang for which my entire social life of 8 years was created. A whole community sprang up around Ylliona, she drew people like a magnet and not desperate, pathological people like I drew. She drew amazing free spirits who worshipped education, travelled the world, were open minded, spoke many languages, had senses of humor, belonged to secret societies, were Wicaans and Warlocks and Communists and spell casters and nudists. I was none of these things really but they accepted me into their fold because Ylliona did and through the osmosis of our fellowship I learned so many things I would have never been exposed to otherwise. It was like a four year university of world studies with no charge.

Ylliona was German and reminded me of Bridget Neilson. She had a short punk haircut, was athletic and took no crap from anyone. I've seen her make sales girls cry. She could be very intimidating and yet be the kindest, most nurturing person on earth. She came to reside over the little community of free spirits and became our default earth mother.

Every Friday night for 8 years we all came together at this little bohemian café called the Tango Tea Room. At first it was just me and Ylliona and Frank and Heather, friends of hers from the university. But then it grew and shifted and changed and so many people came and went I could not keep track of them all. The only thing that stayed constant was me and Ylliona. I had never had friends like this before, mature, intelligent friends whose conversations I could drown in and never want to come up for air. While working at the mall I honestly believe those Friday nights were the only things that kept me sane. It was my only chance for real conversation, the only opportunity to stretch my mind and my beliefs and think outside the confines of culture and tv and the mall.

I began to understand exactly what Dylan was talking about because suddenly for me there was music in the tea room at night and revolution in the air. It was a revolution of the mind, body and spirit. Ylliona took to calling them her coven and the coven became my second family. I felt such love and acceptance and such a true sense of belonging it was almost incomprehensible for an outcast like me to grasp.

It wasn't just the tea room that was my magic carpet, Ylliona's little house across the street from the ocean was like my own personal Mecca. When I did not have a car I would take the bus and from the instant I stepped out, four blocks away, I could feel my pulse calm and my spirit quiet. No matter what was going on in my life, as I walked up those narrow steps to her little loft it all faded into nothingness.

One of the greatest weeks of my life was spent house sitting for her while she was in Germany. She had no phone, no cable and no internet and yet I remember that week like it was a dream. I loved that house. It radiated harmony and tranquility and I can't imagine cross words ever being spoken there.

When I split from my husband Ylliona took me in. I slept on her futon with her fuzzy, ancient black cat whom I was deathly allergic to. In Ylliona's bright living room with its wooden floors and blue fabric draped over the windows, I put on my first and only bikini. It was my favorite color of green and was a Roxy set I could never have afforded in my wildest dreams. I would have never believed I had the body to wear it, but Ylliona did. To prove it she took us to the beach and pointed out every guy that stared our way. It was wonderful and esteem building and spirit renewing beyond all words. I will never forget it as long as I live.

When it disintegrated it was instantaneous. Ylliona gave up her idyllic home on the coast for a little box of a place in the inner city, for what reason I have no idea. She asked everyone to help her move and everyone did, about 20 people showed up, me included. Box by box we took everything from the seashore to the ghetto and into her new place. By this time the universe had taken a dump on me, I had no car, was overweight, working at the redneck electronics store and miserable but I still went and helped out, aggravating an old knee injury that hurt so bad I could barely walk for days. But I was there, I helped because I wanted to, because she was my friend.

Two weeks later we were woken up at three am to our apartment building being on fire. I was terrified and suddenly everything was thrown into limbo. As soon as it was daylight I called and emailed and texted Ylliona. I was so sure she would conscript everyone from her move to help me as well. All she did was tell me not to panic that it couldn't be as bad as what I was making it. I still kept thinking someone would show up to help us out, help us move our things, let us transfer our food to their fridge so $300 worth of groceries we could not afford to buy again would not go to waste. No one did.

But it happened on a Friday so I called her voicemail at the exact time Friday afternoon she would be on her way to the tea room to see the gang. I said "Hey, I know you're on your way to the tea room. Would you please tell everyone we had a fire and we really need help? We have no place to live, we have two days to move all our things to another place and I can't afford to hire movers, we'd really appreciate some help."

No one did. None of Ylliona's gang did. Only Kim and Mark from Mathis, who were only friends of mine on facebook came to our aid. I don't know why Ylliona didn't help and never will. When I had time to come to my senses again I was furious. I posted a long rant on my facebook page to which Ylliona answered and told me everything was my fault, that it wasn't her responsibility to ask anyone to help me when I was too stupid to ask them for help myself. She said I should have hunted down the names, addresses and phone numbers of all 20 of our acquaintances and asked each of them myself and to stop blaming my own incompetence and lack of motivation on her.

When she was sitting at a table surrounded by these people, she could have done the same with two sentences from her mouth. I didn't think that I had to go to such extreme measures to get help when she could just ask for it on my behalf. Obviously I was wrong.

Three weeks later several people called and asked if they could do anything. Three weeks later. By that time there was nothing to be done. We had moved in to another place, bought more food and settled in all on our own and by the grace and help of my sister Toni and Kim and Mark Dionne.

I was never invited out to the tea room again. I was taken off the email list of everyone and no one ever spoke to me again, with the exception of Frank Kelly, whose encouragement was instrumental in helping me get my first book published.

The last time I saw Ylliona was about a month or so after the last time anyone from the group spoke to me. I literally ran into her at the employment office. Like an idiot I somehow thought we were still friends and smiled at her and said "Hey, how ya doing?"

"You still have shit in my house!! You need to get it out! I don't want it there!!" She exploded.

I've never been good at confrontation but confrontation with giant blond angry German women screaming at me is REALLY not my thing. I turned around without a word and went to fax my resume and then went out the back door to avoid running into her. I never saw her again.

Plain White Tease: The girl who called herself Mikey Way

I met her because we both listened to My Chemical Romance. I was writing MCR fan fiction and she was a fan. She got my email and started talking to me and she seemed okay at first. Then things just got strange.

She'd send me these really sexual song lyrics and say they were dedicated to her brother. This really should have been a warning but I kept thinking maybe I was reading something wrong.

Then out of the blue in the middle of a regular email she goes "I told my mom I was raped and she didn't do anything about it, just offered to get me a therapist". I asked her WTF and she pretended she didn't say anything.

Then she told me her brother had been raping her since she was in the 5th grade.

Then she told me he got her hooked on drugs.

She told me he beat her all the time.

Then she told me he got her pregnant when she was 15.

Then she told me she was anorexic because he was always telling her how fat she was. She claimed she was so anorexic she miscarried his baby and it was so bad the doctors told her she'd never be able to have children.

Then she told me she was in love with him.

Then she told me she had two younger sisters and if she didn't let him rape her, he'd be raping them.

She claimed she told her parents and they did nothing. She claimed her pastor told her she was going to hell.

This was over a period of about four YEARS. In the process of all this she got real possessive with me.

If I did not stay on line and chat with her for HOURS at a time EVERY SINGLE NIGHT, she threatened to kill herself.

She started calling herself Mikey and me Gerard (after the brothers in MCR) and referred to herself as my brother. At first I thought it was cute, like a term of endearment, but considering she was supposedly having sex with her brother the whole time…I'm not so sure that was a good thing.

She faked a suicide attempt once and let me think she was dead for four days.

She told me if I did not email and chat with her on a daily basis and tell her to eat she would starve herself.

If I talked about anyone else, any other friends, she threw tantrums and threatened to kill herself.

When two other girls, The girl who loved Jade Puget and The generic scene girl from Austin, I knew from online came to visit one summer she claimed to run off with a meth dealer and sell herself to him for drugs.

Then she told me her brother had gone off to fight in Iraq.

Then things got REALLY freaky. She started fighting with me, ALL the time. Calling me names, starting fights for the sake of arguing for NO reason at all. If I said the sky was blue, she'd say it was green.

She claimed she was coming to see me, even gave me names, dates, places. Waited for me to take off from work and rent a car to meet her and then said "Yes, I'm coming to Texas, no I'm not coming to see you because you were never worth my time." She was always fucking with me for the simple reason that she could. And really because I let her.

She started stalking me to other sites.
I started blocking her finally.

I should have done this YEARS before but I felt bad for her, I gave her the benefit of the doubt and thought maybe there was SOMETHING I could do on my end that would help her.

A year passed.
She wrote me on myspace and told me her brother had been killed in Iraq. I said "Well at least now you know he'll never hurt another little girl ever again."
She FREAKED out and tole me I was cold and unforgiving and didn't deserve to live, and I was going to hell but her brother was in heaven.
I blocked her again.
Another year passed.

She changed email and contacted me and told me she'd been engaged to 4 different guys, all in her brother's Marine unit and had married his best friend who looked exactly like him. And she was pregnant.

When I reminded her that she had told me she couldn't have kids, she immediately wrote back and said she'd miscarried.

I tried AGAIN and for a while she was okay and was nice.

Then I started catching her in all these lies. Apparently enough time had passed that she didn't remember all the things she told me. Then she started fighting with me again.

Finally I said "This is it. I cannot believe anything else you tell me. I am going to list for you all the things you have claimed happened to you in the last six years and all the hateful things you said to me, all the times I tried to help you, went out of my way to help you. You need to own up to all the shit you've said, done and never once apologized for."

I blocked her AGAIN. I blocked her on every site I thought she was on.
EXCEPT facebook.

She stalked me to facebook and sent me a message saying "Yes I lied, I lied about everything for six years. But only to you because you deserved it. My brother never did a thing to me. I made it all up. You're a horrible excuse for a human being, don't EVER contact me again."

I loved The Girl Who Called Herself Mikey Way. I loved her as if she had come from my own body, I loved her for six years and for her to say that everything she'd ever told me for six years was made up just to pass the time, because she could and because I was easy to fuck with and gullible was just DEVASTATING,

The "I hate you and want to get back at you and can't believe you did that" phase is over and I'm just left being sad.

There is an apartment complex behind the mall I pass a lot because the street its on is less crowded than getting on the freeway. I remember telling The Girl Who Called Herself Mikey Way if she would just run away and come down here I'd take her in, give her a job at the mall, when I ran my own place there, and I'd help her to rent an apartment in that complex so she'd live just across the street. And even though Axl Rosebush and I were barely getting by, I meant it and I would have gone hungry and broke trying to fulfill it had she actually shown up, had anything she told me been the truth. The fact that she made me believe she would come down and live and go to school here one day really just hurts.

Shin Solo/Rachel:
One of the "AFI girls" was someone who called herself Shin Solo. Just like the other kids I deemed "AFI girls" we met through our love of the band and I came to know, love and trust her as if she was part of my family. We met through my writing on fandomination.net and were friends for about four years.

As we were becoming friends, she told me first how when she was in high school her boyfriend had beaten her all the time, she had gotten pregnant from him and lost the baby when he beat her so bad she was put in the hospital. When she woke up she said she told her mother and her mother simply said "Yeah I always knew what was going on because you looked scared every time he came in the room." Initially I was horrified, and much like with The girl who called herself Mikey Way I thought I could save her, make her better, make her whole and love and encourage her enough that it would make up for whatever happened in her life. However those bad things she said had happened to her, seemed to happen every week.

She would later say the same thing about every single boyfriend she had. She would later say the same thing about every guy she ever met period.

Two years after the last time we spoke she dropped off the face of the earth. She stopped responding to emails. The last I had heard she was straightedge, living in the dorms at the University of Memphis, on the Dean's list and doing well.

Then nothing.

Earlier in the year RIGHT AT THE EXACT TIME my apt burned down she got back a hold of me and told me she had been working as a phone sex operator and then a prostitute and THAT'S why she hadn't spoken to me. This girl's life was nothing but drama, the only time she got a hold of me was to tell me some guy beat her up or raped her which seemed to happen every time she walked out her door.

Of course by this time I got some distance I was pretty much done with the drama and had enough of my own.

When I told her it was a shame she let her education go she told me oh no, she had been homeless and a phone sex operator and a prostitute AND STILL had graduated with honors. But even though the college had a computer lab she still couldn't contact me to let me know if she was alive or dead. Whatever. I didn't fall right in with the drama and didn't act sympathetic so she cussed me out and said "I don't have to justify myself to you!" and that was it.

She popped up again, asking me to send her some My Chemical Romance fan fics (the ones I had written with and for the girl who called herself Mikey Way) because it was the reason we met and she missed me. I was feeling a bit more charitable so I accepted the email and sort of said "Look, I keep to myself, I don't get in other people's business, I'm glad you're alive, I feel bad for telling you to leave me alone but I can't be involved in your problems."

Two days later I get a three page email about every single thing she had done in the last year, even though I had asked not to be told. On she ranted about THE PHONE SEX STUFF, THE GUYS SHE'S FUCKED, THE PROSTITUTION, THE DRUGS SHE'S DONE, THE DRINKING, THE HANGOVERS, THE TIMES SHE WAS BEATEN, THE TIMES SHE WAS RAPED, SHE WAS KNOCKED UP AND FORCED TO HAVE AN ABORTION, plus ten million other people and stories and stuff I had NO idea about in all this detail…
None of which I asked about in ANY way, shape or form.

I did not react to any of this because 1) I don't believe any of it. 2) you can't just ignore me for two years, come back for a day and do that!!

Then she starts talking about how I inspired her and how she wants to be edge again. She's already broken edge AT LEAST TWICE that I know of, plus she told me she only became edge because she was obsessed with AFI.

OK—YOU DO NOT BRAG TO A STRAIGHTEDGE PERSON ABOUT ALL THE DRUGS YOU'VE DONE, GUYS YOU'VE FUCKED (FOR MONEY NO LESS) AND THEN TURN AROUND AND SAY "Oh I can't wait to be edge again." IT DOES NOT WORK THAT WAY.
IT IS A VOW YOU TAKE FOR LIFE.
IF YOU LEAVE IT, YOU LEAVE IT.
PERIOD.
Well this was not enough to get a rise out of me either. I knew she only said it to get a reaction and I wasn't going to give her one.

She then goes on about how her mom (whom she previously claimed was a drug addict who beat her and did nothing when she was beaten so badly by her boyfriend she miscarried—supposedly) and how they are now best friends and her mom was so much more supportive than I had been.

I don't react. I say "Enjoy it while you can. My mom's dead. I'll never get that chance."

THEN SHE TELLS ME HOW TWO NIGHTS AGO SHE WAS KIDNAPPED AND RAPED ON HER WAY HOME FROM DOING LAUNDRY!!

Not getting a reaction any other way, she fell back into what she knew best: pretending to be raped.

Finally I wrote back and told her "I am not mad, I do not hold it against you but we can't go back to how things were. I am not a cop or a therapist, I cannot help you with your problems. There was a time when I tried, there was a time when I loved you and you threw that away. Time has passed and I can't go back. I don't want to hear your problems. I don't know you anymore and it is very possible that I never did."

Several years back I met a girl who knew Shin in real life and told me EVERYTHING she'd ever told me was made up. I don't even know how we met but I remember going "Oh my god, she just dropped off the face of the earth and I don't know if she's dead or locked up or what?" (she had also claimed to have been declared legally insane by the state of Tennessee).

The girl said "Oh no, she just started fucking some new guy and when she did she ditched all her friends. Don't feel bad, you're not the only one she bailed on".

When I mentioned all the shit she had been through the girl responded with "Oh god, you do know all the shit she ever told you was made up, right?"

And of course no, that actually never occurred to me. I loved her, I trusted her and how could someone lie about being raped anyway?

I told this to Rachel. I said "You're not straightedge anymore, that's fine. I'm glad you and your mom are getting along. I don't want to know these things about you anymore. I'm not mad, I don't hate you but I also don't believe you."

So she wrote back, cussed me out AGAIN (she cussed me out the first time for taking her off my friends list on facebook and myspace the first time when I told her to get lost) and proclaimed: "That girl who said she knew me is only 15, how can you believe a 15 year old over me? And no she doesn't know me in real life I've been having cyber-sex with her for the last five years. That's it!" She then demanded to know how I knew the girl, how many times I had spoken to her and exactly what she had said to me.

I did some quick calculations and responded with "Well if that is true you were having cyber-sex with a 10 year old when you were 18 and that's child pornography and that makes you a pedophile. I also answered her questions and told her what the girl had told me and if she hadn't known her in real life she did know her much better than I did.

That did it. She didn't respond to anything else I had said about the girl or how she knew her or whether or not she had lied to me for the last five years.

Instead, she wrote back an email that said "YOU'RE CRAZY!! WHY ARE YOU DOING THIS TO ME? WHY DID YOU CONTACT ME?! YOU'RE HARASSING ME! STOP EMAILING ME AND LEAVE ME ALONE!!".

She was the one who started it with me and I didn't know that expecting the truth was harassment.

She popped up one more time and wanted to know how she could buy my book. I went ahead and blocked her after that on the advice of my SANE friends who are my own age. I still miss her and wish I could have saved her. I don't doubt something horrible happened to her that made her the way she is now. Very likely she was raped or traumatized by someone she loved and trusted and no one was there to help her. However she chooses to relive it over and over again or maybe to actually live in her mind where she believed it was true, and pulls it out like something from a bag of tricks when she feels she isn't getting the attention she deserves. I wish I could have helped her, I wish I had known how.

THE AFI GIRLS

The Girl Who Loved Jade Puget and The generic scene girl from Austin were chronicled earlier here. The Girl Who Loved Jade Puget and The generic scene girl from Austin are not their real names. I don't remember The Girl Who Loved Jade Puget's name, if what she gave me was even real, and The generic scene girl from Austin changed hers when she came into her trust fund and stopped being my friend. If either of them read this, you've done enough to cause me pain, don't sue me.

Meeting each of them face to face the first time was like standing face to face with parts of myself from other times in my life. They each had their own sad stories to lay on me. The generic scene girl from Austin lost her mom at the same age I did. She said she was bi, like me, but leaning more toward gay, said she was straightedge, like me. We attended the same AFI show in Austin, neither knowing the other was there. It was the first time each of us had seen them. What The Generic Scene Girl From Austin did not tell me was that she was a trust fund baby who was just killing time until she came into her cache. For four years she sent me letters, visited, called me on the phone and emailed, chatted and shared journal entries with me online. She told me she loved me, she called me her hero, she said she would have killed herself if she hadn't me and that I saved her. I was dumb enough to believe it all. I had seen Schindler's List and really believed that if I saved one person I saved the world entire. I really wanted to save the world.

She came into her fortune, changed her name, informed she had a boyfriend and told me to never contact her again. This only lasted until she would run into me at the last AFI show I attended, again in Austin. She made a big deal of coming up, hugging me, crying, introducing herself to my friends. When I emailed her after the show she told me to get lost.

The The Girl Who Loved Jade Puget story is exactly the same only with a few variations on the details. She claimed to be gay, claimed to be straightedge, claimed to have a mom who was an alcoholic who would take up with any man who would pay her bills. I helped pay for her to come visit me in Texas twice, both times using money I did not have that threw me into debt. She told me she would kill herself if I did not find a way to get her out of her house, kill herself or run away to a life on the streets. I believed her.

The last time I ever saw her was on Friday the 13th. I was to drive the girl who loved Jade Puget back to Austin to meet The Generic Scene Girl From Austin. Along the way they had become best friends. I was an extra in my own life again, unloved, unneeded, crowded out. I have no idea why The Girl Who Loved Jade Puget came to see me that one last time when she could have spent her entire summer break with The generic scene girl from Austin. I am not superstitious but driving her across the state on Friday the 13th scared me.

The previous year on Friday the 13th I'd gotten into a terrible car wreck. I did not want that to happen again. Still I wanted to get some entertainment value out of it for The Girl Who Loved Jade Puget who seemed more and more unimpressed with the places we had gone that summer than the one before. I took her to a Mexican Curio shop, a place of spells, idols, charms and potions in a genuinely creepy setting and bought a good luck candle. It was the same candle you could get at any dollar store but supposedly it had the blessing of…well, I don't know. Someone important I guess. The night before our trip we lit it.

I took her to Austin and she hugged me then ran to The Generic Scene Girl From Austin like the hounds of hell were after her and I never saw her again. Did it truly bring me luck? Well, we didn't crash, we weren't killed, but after I spent more money than I ever had on her visit, which she thanked me for with robot like fake sincerity, I never saw her and she never spoke to me again.

I still remember the night before she left. I was exhausted from work but she wanted me to take her around to see some sights at night. The best sight to see at night in Corpus is the Lex. We drove over the Harbor Bridge at night singing along to Thursdays' Ashes of American Flags. I normally don't sing around people because my voice makes small dogs implode but I sang with The Girl Who Loved Jade Puget because I loved and trusted her. I can still see she and I standing next to the World War II aircraft carrier USS Lexington which is moored in Corpus Christi Bay at 11 o'clock at night. All the stars were out, the ship was shrouded in the azure light that earned it the name The Blue Ghost. The sand looked grey beneath our feet, the ocean was black and the caps of the waves were white. Above us the Blue Ghost loomed frighteningly large and ominous and we felt small in the universe.

My husband and I were on the verge of splitting then and The Girl Who Loved Jade Puget refused to sleep over with him in the house. So I wrote a hot check for $200 to put him up in a hotel, on top of the hot checks I had written to get her food and take her around because the minute she got into my car she announced she had left most of her money with The Generic Scene Girl From Austin. I didn't mind though, I wanted to spoil her because I was so sure if I didn't, no one else would. If it ruined me in the process so be it. That was in 2007, and the grocery store chain HEB still will not take a check on me.

I wasn't planning on spending so much for a motel for my husband. It just so happened there was a 4 H convention in town and every motel and hotel was booked. I had to take my husband almost all the way out of town to find him a room and the only one available was very expensive. When I got back home The Girl Who Love Jade Puget announced she did not want to sleep in the same bed with me even if I slept on top of the covers, even if the bed was more than big enough for the two of us. So I took the floor and gave her the bed. But I do not like to think about that her being a stereotypical selfish teenager. I prefer to think of the ride over the Harbor Bridge and the Blue Ghost like a phantom on the cresting waves under the moonlight.

Sometimes remembering it hurts so bad it was like my heart had its own set of ribs and one by one they were being snapped inside me. I have since made my peace with the Harbor Bridge. My heart no longer aches when I have to drive over it going to and from work three days a week

On the drive home to Corpus alone I had plenty of time to think. Sadness and emptiness and hurt gave way to this really odd feeling of pride and accomplishment. That feeling lasted for about two hours before I sank into unfathomable depression that lasted for years.

All I ever wanted for The Girl Who Loved Jade Puget and the generic scene girl from Austin was for them to have strength, stability, independence, and to grow up and leave the troubles of their adolescence far behind. And that's exactly what they did in a roundabout way, without a look back or a thank you. When they left their teenage years behind, they also left me behind too. And in finding strength and wisdom and surety on their own, they would no longer need me for anything. I'm not sure what I expected, maybe that they would be like real daughters, always around to support and care for and comfort me. Much like I once romanticized what being straightedge was, I must have romanticized what it might be like to have children as well. Maybe you just give and they take and then you die and there is no reward, no saving the world, nothing but memories.

I tried to throw away every remnant of their friendship, but some things I could not part with. In the very back of my closet there is a pile of letters I keep just to convince myself I did not imagine the whole experience. On one visit the Girl Who Loved Jade Puget gave me a rubber ducky for the tub. That rubber duck has followed me to three different apartments. Who throws away a rubber ducky? It's so cute and smiley, I just don't have the heart. I don't use it either. It sits on the edge of my tub collecting dust.

The winter after my dad died I found the greatest jacket in the world in a store in Odessa that has since closed down. It's a bomber jacket with a Texas flag taking up the entire back of the jacket. It cost two hundred and fifty dollars and at age twenty it was the single most expensive thing I had ever bought for myself. I don't have the occasion to wear it much in Corpus, much like Tom Cruise it stays in the closet. At some point the Girl Who Loved Jade Puget wrote me a letter that I opened and read on the bus going to work. I folded the letter and put it in the inner pocket of the jacket. That was probably sometime in 2003. It is still there. Once every year or so I put the jacket on, I stop for a moment wondering what is in the lining of my jacket, right next to my heart. Then I remember and I leave it exactly where it is at.

I have learned that "Family" is not the term I thought it was.
Family
The concept has always mystified me. It has been confusing, terrifying, and something I have never been able to get a good handle on.

For the longest time it was programmed into me that you had to love your family members because…well they were your family—like it was predestined, like it was meant to be.

Maybe it is like that and maybe it is different with big families, filled with siblings close in age, or families that still have both parents alive.

This was never the case with me. Growing up I would try to explain to friends and classmates that I had no "real" brothers and sisters, only "half" brothers and sisters. Back in the 1970s when I was in school (yes, I'm old) no one got this, they looked at me like I was nuts. I'd try to explain that both my parents were married before and I was the only child they had together. As time went on and what constituted a family had looser boundaries, more people understood, but in grade school I was a freak.

I was the youngest, the last, the only one my mom and dad had together and quite possibly a huge mistake. I never fit in with the other members of my family. I didn't just feel awkward around them, being around them was terrifying. It was like being in a foreign country where I didn't know the language. We were so different. I used to fantasize that I was adopted and became obsessed with the fact when I could not come up with one single photo of my mom pregnant with me. Later on though I found birth announcements and birth certificates and I guess it had to be true. Looking back I can see how I get parts of myself from my mom and parts from my dad, both of whom are long since dead so I can't ask them about any of these traits. However this never kept me from feeling like I was from another planet when it came to the rest of my family.

I tried, unsuccessfully, for thirty five years, to fit in with them. Sometimes I think it would have been vastly easier to have grown up an orphan with no family at all than to have one where I was shunned and so clearly didn't fit in.

I can piece together things that no one had to tell me but I could pretty much ascertain on my own, like the fact that my mom probably never had a relationship in her life in which she was not abused. She came from a family of very smart people and yet never finished high school b/c of being pregnant with my oldest sister.

My oldest sister was never right in the head. She loved mayhem. She was never happy unless she was causing other members of my family to be at each other's throats. Her daughter lost one of her eyes and grew up in foster care due to my sister's negligence. When my sister was bored she'd go and have sex with the husbands of my other sisters. Half sisters, I mean. She killed herself when she was sixty. Yet everyone loved her and everyone hated me. I was not invited to her funeral. The only reason I was called at all was because they had the misguided impression that I had somehow gotten rich and they wanted me to pay for the funeral for a woman I never knew who only interacted with me three times in my life and two of those times were only to spread rumors about me. I couldn't pay for the funeral so I wasn't invited.

My brother has a facebook account filled with photos of himself and this sister. He has spoken to me twice since I was 16 and never accepted my friends request when I found him on facebook.

The things one would do to be accepted into my family were things I could not stomach: do drugs, get arrested, sleep with many men/women, go to jail, date convicts, wed drug dealers, have abortions. When my mom was dying and I was 8 years old and being shuffled back and forth, even then I was appalled at their living conditions and what passed for homes. I remember one of my sisters commenting that whenever I came to visit I always cleaned her house. It wasn't out of courtesy, it was out of necessity: the place was like a cesspool. It made my skin crawl and yet she lived there, like an animal, in the midst of it, and never knew the difference.

I tried so hard to fit in, to make them love me, to make them proud. The only time they took any interest in me at all was when something bad happened to me.

I went through many phases of wanting others, unrelated, to be my family. I chose never to have children. Not having had parents, how would I know how to raise them? And I'd be damned if I'd let them grow up feeling as lost and unloved as I had.

I worked at a mall for 10 years and began to try and foster kids. I met over 80 kids in 10 years. They all called me mom. But they all left and went their separate ways for better or worse. Some used me for anything they could get: money, food, clothes, attention. Others asked nothing but didn't need me for nearly as long as I needed them.

Eight years ago I became straightedge and learned that those of us who claim this lifestyle call each other "brother" and "sister". I was elated. I was so sure then that I had found the family I never had. But no one took it as seriously as I did for very long. I met hundreds of people in 8 years and only about four of them are still my "brothers" and "sisters", which means I lost hundreds of "family" just like losing my own. And it didn't hurt any less either.

Finally, in my middle age, it hit me: I am not a member of a family. I never was. I was born with a certain blood type, a certain strand of DNA, that happens to match that of five or six total strangers. I am alone. That is simply the way it is and it will never change.

Oddly, thanks to facebook, I found my dad had several more children I was not aware of and I have more strangers out there that share my DNA, or at least a tiny part of it. That does not make them any more special than any other of the 500+ "friends" I have. It just means Dad couldn't keep it in his pants.

Accepting this comes with freedom, much like accepting your fate with a terminal illness. I don't have a family. I never did. I don't know where I came from or why I was born. That's okay. It has to be because it is something I cannot change.

"I am unique
Therefore I am alone" Data on Star Trek

I will never have children, I prefer the company of hermit crabs, stray cats (and not the band, though I still wouldn't kick Brian Setzer out of bed), and my students. However I got all the experience of being a parent in six or seven years rather than eighteen and the scars were not on my stomach but on my heart. I am not blameless in all of this. I hold everyone to my standards. I expect loyalty and compassion and I expect them to either lead a good clean life, or if not, not to come bragging to me about a life I do not understand and cannot condone. I am sure in each instance I did something to drive these people away, make them loathe me. I was too chatty or too silent, smothered them or never told them I loved them enough, judged them too harshly or somehow made them feel unwanted, when all I really wanted was not to be stepped on or used. I lost all of them, but I still hope they come back. Like the Carly Simon song says, if you're willing to make that change, it will be coming around again. I hope I have changed into a better person. I love them all, I pray for them at night and fall asleep into dreams where they are still my friends, my spirit daughters, my progeny and I am still loved and still somebody's hero.

EPILOGUE: POEMS REPRESENTATIVE OF MY LIFE

THIS IS THE NEW BLOOD

Today I am giving away some sXe gear
Not because I broke
God no
Because I am too fat for it and I am giving it to
the next generation.
Because I want to share my story with someone who understands.
Because I want to give it to someone who deserves it.
Because I gave all my other shirts
to people who broke and I want to break the cycle
of people taking my edge shirts only to break edge
and piss on everything they stood for.
Because I am so proud of you
and if I had a daughter, Kerra
I'd want it to be you.

The mall has changed completely
almost everything is gone
Becky, the one I always referred to as
"That cute lil goth girl"
is here with us.
She is your mom.
I remember her buying you an AFI bag
for back to school
when you were in the sixth grade.
Everything has changed yet here we are.

"Well"
I begin
it is a story I can repeat in my sleep

yet I am telling it to you and that makes it unique
"The first straightedge boy I ever knew
was this guy named Christopher
He worked right there at Hot Topic, right there."
Hot Topic is now right behind us
and the food court, where we are sitting,
is downstairs.
"and he looked like a REALLY skinny Henry Rollins
He wore Buddy Holly glasses and I thought he was so cute.
And I said something to someone and they told me
"Oh he wouldn't even talk to YOU
he's straightedge and vegan"
and so I looked up what straightedge was
and realized it was something
I had been my whole life before I was 20.
And he would always come to work wearing AFI shirts
and one day I said "Chris, what does AFI stand for?"
and that was it."
You're grinning.
"So it took me several years of mulling it over
before I realized that's what I wanted for my life
By the time I made my commitment
he was long gone from the mall.
So I had someone try and track him down online
and I found out the band he was in was promoting
clothes for this clothing company.
So I found their site and bought
$100 worth of shirts
and that Christmas I gave them
to every straightedge friend I had
And every single one of them broke edge
within the first year.
This was my favorite shirt
It was limited edition."
I hand you what was one time my most prized possession.

It is a black t shirt with yellow lettering.
It says STRAIGHT EDGE:
FIGHT UNTIL DEATH FOR A DRUG FREE NATION.
I ordered two of these shirts in this design, my favorite,
I gave one away to a the girl I used to call The girl who loved Jade Puget
She broke edge on New Years Eve 2007.
After she broke edge, she never spoke to me again.
All my pride and honor and hope
all the crazy things I've ever done in the past six years
has been sweated into the fabric of this shirt.
This shirt is now yours.
I can tell you're crying.
"I bought these yellow and black earrings to go with the shirt."
I hand you my earrings.
"Now the band he was in was like
the straightedge hardcore version
of the Khumbia Kings.
If you found a guy in Corpus that was edge
he was probably a member of The Contender
This brings me to the next shirt.
There was a clothing company out of Austin called Still Here.
Ironically, they're not.
They went out of business.
They were one of the first places I ever bought edge clothing from.
Well they went out of business and when they did
the owner sent out an email to everyone saying
'By now I bet you guys aren't even edge anymore and you
probably think this whole thing is stupid but I wanted
to write each of you and thank you for supporting us in the past.'
and it just made me so sad
so I wrote him back and said
"I'M STILL EDGE, I don't think this is stupid at all."
He wrote back and said "Oh you're from Corpus,
well I was in The Contender!"
We start laughing.

"That's where I bought the SUPPORT LEFTIST HARDCORE shirt I
wore to AFI and that's where I bought this."
I give you the second shirt.
"And this is a Casey Jones shirt I bought that was too small to begin with
but I figured I'd just hang it up on my wall."
"Oh my god, this is so hardcore!"
You are grinning and crying at the same time.
I hand you the book and tell you how proud I am of you
You open it and read the inscription
while your mom tells me how, from the day you knew
what straightedge was, you knew it was for you
and you never wavered even though you had opportunities to break.
You pull out the stickers.
I forgot to mention those,
I got those from Still Here too.
As much as I want a sXe sticker on our car
Axl Rosebush drives it to go buy beer.
I can't put an edge sticker on a car
with beer in it.
It wouldn't be right.
So I give them to you
and you exclaim that this is exactly
what you want your chest piece to look like
I am thinking now of my friend Amy
and how I must introduce you two on facebook
because she has a KILLER chest piece
and she's edge.
And we are hugging and taking pictures
and I am so proud of you
joking with Becky that I would gladly
claim you as mine and take credit for all her hard work.
And then at sunset
we stroll back through the mall
the place where I met your mom
and I met the straightedge boy

who is now a straightedge man
just as I am an old straightedge woman
and I will take this to my grave
and I will never have a daughter
yet I am so proud of you
and we hug some more and part ways

I think of you as my own
my straightedge vegan socialist militant hardcore daughter
of whom I am very proud and love very much.

DIONYSUS SLEEPS IN ICE

for Rosa and Kim, and yes Kim I took the title from your poem
Dionysus Sleeps In Gin

Dionysus no longer speaks to me
so I am thinking of you now my friends
in faraway places
all who have come and gone
because December is the month of deaths
and vast emptiness hollowed out like
rotting jack o'lanterns come November
I never stopped loving them
no matter what they did to me
and I am thinking of you now
drinking pumpkin spice tea
and thinking how you will leave me too
but I am selfish
and keep you all locked in
the icy bone cell of my heart
frozen in the cold white amber
of the last time
you said you loved me

THE GIRL WHO CALLED HERSELF MIKEY WAY
COLLABORATION WITH KIM ACRYLIC

She holds conversations with ancient mimes
falling from her dreams she becomes manmade: synthetic
bruised by her kisses you run into the silver rain
crumbled in the ruin of your body you spar your madness
losing only to the broken bottles of intoxications

You will never forget her insanity
that pulled you in and taught you to love
You sleep with her lies and try to make
them into a reality you could touch
It never happens
They crumble in your hands
sugar cookie crystals falling from the sun

Journey to the center of your silicone dream
make believe hand puppets become your best friends
where is the future in outer space?
I free form my life, Shirley she will see the metaphors
i kiss your soberly toned lips caressing your past diseases
falling up hills, knees scabbed with superficial rejection I fail...

She starts to short circuit
the plastic warps and red turns to faded pink
as she winds to a halt the sounds are so sad
the carousel jingle slowing to a whine
goodbye automated angelic girl
girl who talked to ghosts
my polyester princess
(c) Kim-Hoff Acrylic and Joey Jabor Luke 2010

BUY BOTH OF OUR BOOKS AT
WWW.PUBLISHAMERICA.COM